Queen of the Cosmos

The cross on Mt Krizevac.

Queen of the Cosmos

JAN CONNELL

Introduction by Robert Faricy, S.J.

PARACLETE PRESS
Orleans, Massachusetts

Declaration

The decree of the Congregation for the Propagation of the Faith, A.A.S. 58, 1186 (Approved by Pope Paul VI on October 14, 1966) states that the **Nihil Obstat** and **Imprimatur** are no longer required on publications that deal with private revelations, provided that they contain nothing contrary to faith and morals. The author wishes to manifest her unconditional submission to the final and official judgment of the Magisterium of the Church, regarding the events presently under investigation at Medjugorje.

1st Printing,   *May 1990*
2nd Printing,   *July 1990*
3rd Printing,   *January 1991*
4th Printing,   *September 1991*
5th Printing,   *January 1992*
6th Printing,   *May 1992*
7th Printing,   *November 1992*

ISBN: 1-55725-018-9
Printed in the United States of America

In the name of
the Lord Jesus Christ,
this work is dedicated to
the Holy Trinity
and consecrated to
the Eternal Father,
through the inspiration of
the Holy Spirit.

Editor's Note

When I first went to Medjugorje, I was filled with skepticism. Why Mary? Why Medjugorje? Was it real? Or the ultimate deception of the Angel of Light at the end of the age? Jesus' words to His disciples were much in mind: "A good tree cannot bring forth evil fruit, neither can an evil tree bring forth good fruit." (Matt. 7:18)

What I found in Medjugorje was a profound, on-going spiritual awakening, not just in the village but throughout the countryside. And it was spreading all over the world, as pilgrims returned home, determined to live out what they had experienced. In many of the people there, was a sweet humility and a selfless charity. They did not say much; their lives spoke for them.

Recently I heard ecumenism explained: walk in my steps awhile. Suffer a little of what I suffer for what I treasure, and perhaps you will see why I treasure it. I was privileged to spend some time with a few of the Visionaries. I found them to be normal and healthy, handling an extremely stressful assignment with much grace. It is not any assignment that anyone would envy. I also found them to be without guile. The fruit is good.

Which means that God is doing an extraordinary thing in Medjugorje. He has sent Mary to these humblest of circumstances, to re-introduce His Son to the world. She is calling us—not just Catholics, all of us—to return to Him. Indeed, words like "Catholic" and "Protestant" have little meaning, as we kneel at the foot of the Cross. There, we are one.

—*David Manuel*

Contents

St James Church, Medjugorje.

Introduction

Robert Faricy, SJ

Fr. Faricy is professor of Spiritual Theology at the Pontifical Gregorian University, Rome, Italy. An American Jesuit, he is a graduate of the United States Naval Academy and a native of Minnesota.

On June 24th, 1981, the Blessed Virgin Mary appeared to two young girls, Mirjana Dragicevic and Ivanka Ivankovic, as they were walking along the outskirts of the village of Medjugorje in central Yugoslavia. Ivanka, noticing first, said to Mirjana, "Look what's up there on the hill!" They saw a brilliant light and in it a shining figure. Ivanka said, "Mirjana, could it be the Blessed Mother?"

Mirjana waved her hand and said, "Come on! You think She would appear to us?" And frightened, they ran away.

The next day the two girls returned with several of their friends. Again the shining figure appeared, and began speaking. This time, in addition to the two girls, three other teenagers and a little boy saw her and heard her. She identified herself as the

Blessed Mother, and returned to them the following day. To four of the six Visionaries, as they came to be called, she has continued to appear every day. Since in 1981 Yugoslavia was under oppressive Communist rule and officially atheistic, the Government was furious. People were put in prison, including the first pastor, Fr. Jozo Zovko, O.F.M., because of their loyalty to the apparitions of the Blessed Mother. The six young people were threatened, verbally and physically, by the local police, and the Government did many terrible things. Nevertheless, right from the beginning, those who go to the Medjugorje apparitions experience the power of God's love coming through the Blessed Virgin Mary.

Nine years later, the Blessed Virgin Mary is still appearing, though no longer daily to all six. Ivanka, now in her early twenties, is married and a mother. The Blessed Virgin appears to her once or twice a year. Mirjana, who has graduated from the University of Sarajevo and is now married, is visited by the Blessed Mother on the second day of each month, and annually on her birthday. But the other four Visionaries continue to see her every day. One of them, Vicka, was quite sick for several years. The Blessed Virgin Mary promised she would be healed on September 25, 1988, and she was. Jacov, who was ten years old at the time of the first apparition, now works in the parish bookstore. The other boy, Ivan, has been in the army, doing his military service. Since his discharge, he has visited the United States and other places, before returning to Medjugorje.

Marija has also been to the United States. In December of 1988, at the University of Alabama Hospital, she donated a kidney to her brother who was mortally ill. On the 25th day of every month Marija receives a special message from the Blessed Virgin Mary for the parish of Medjugorje and for the whole world.

What is the attitude of the Church toward Medjugorje? The attitude of the pastor of the parish and of the priests there, as well as that of the sisters, has always been positive. All of the theologians whom I know who have any expertise in this area believe in the authenticity of these apparitions. We believe Mary is actually appearing and speaking.

In Rome and elsewhere, it is general knowledge that the Pope is favorable toward the apparitions at Medjugorje. In 1988, he told Bishop Murilo Krieger of Santa Caterina, Brazil: "Medjugorje is a great center of spirituality," and he encourages people to go there. When they return home, he urges all, including bishops, to practice whatever they have learned at Medjugorje. He has personally convened a commission of Yugoslavian bishops to investigate the authenticity of the apparitions of Medjugorje—the first time a Pontiff has ever done so. The Bishops' Commission is now weighing the evidence, and it is possible that Medjugorje will be approved as a place of pilgrimage while the apparitions are occurring. If it is, that, too, will be a first.

Numerous phenomena associated with the apparitions at Medjugorje have been reported. The sick are being healed. People are seeing extraordinary effects in the sun. The metal parts of rosaries are turning gold. We theologians have a certain amount of trouble with such phenomena. Yet I have seen rosaries which have changed color, and I have looked directly at the sun in Medjugorje and have seen it seem to spin and turn different colors. It would be easier to report that it is just hysteria—except that I would then have to accuse myself of being hysterical, which I was not. As for the healings, they are numerous, medically documented, and currently under investigation.

What have these phenomena to do with faith? They are wonders by which God signs His handiwork, but they are not central to the apparitions. God has sent Mary, the Mother of Jesus, to call us to repent and turn to Him, and to receive the Lord's love in our life. That is at the center. Never in the history of Christianity has the Blessed Virgin Mary appeared to so many people over so long a period of time with such regularity. Moreover, it seems that the apparitions at Medjugorje have ushered in a new Marian age. There are reports of her appearing everywhere— in Africa, in Ecuador, in the Ukraine, in southern Italy, in Argentina, in Arizona. . . . And a number of these reports appear to be authentic; their messages are remarkably similar to the messages being received at Medjugorje. Yet one must remain cautious, for there are also hundreds of false apparitions.

What is the Blessed Virgin Mary saying? First, she is calling us to Conversion. She is calling us to turn from sin—from sinful relationships, habits, behavior, from gossip, back-biting, laziness, whatever our sins are—and turn to God. We are to make Him, not ourselves, the center of our life .

The second point is Faith. We are called to turn to God with faith—not faith that simply believes that Jesus is Savior or a loving and powerful Lord; faith that holds onto Him and has a personal relationship with Him in prayer.

That is the third point: Prayer. As part of her message, Mary frequently urges us to "pray, pray, pray!" She is calling us to prayer, especially the rosary—to contemplative prayer, silent prayer, making visits to churches, being silent before the Lord. She is calling us to frequent Mass, and to frequent confession, which is a sacramental form of prayer, as is the Mass.

She is also calling us to Penance, especially to fasting. We must do it according to our health, the kind of work we do, and our age, but we are all called to fast. Nor is the fasting limited to special days. In Medjugorje she has called for fasting on bread and water on Wednesdays and Fridays, the traditional days of fast. But we are all called to fast sometime—from food, from smoking, from coffee, from something. It might be some other form of indulgence, or perhaps an attitude—if you pray, you will know what God is calling you to set aside.

The result of our efforts is Peace. If we are converted to a closer union with God in faith, if we live out our faith, especially in a prayerful relationship with the Lord, and if we do penance, especially fasting, then we will have peace in our hearts. We will have peace in our family and community, and there will be more peace in the world.

There is a great urgency underlying these messages from Medjugorje. The Blessed Virgin Mary is calling us to conversion now—for she knows what awaits us. She has told the Visionaries that she will impart to them ten secrets concerning the future of the world. The two girls who no longer see her daily, Ivanka and Mirjana, have already received all ten. The others have been given nine. When they receive the tenth secret, it is probable that they, too, will no longer see Mary on a daily basis.

Of the secrets, we know that they consist, in part at least, of predictions of very serious things that are going to happen in the world. The first two things are warnings. The third secret is some kind of permanent sign that Mary is going to leave on the hill of Podbrdo (Apparition Hill), where she first appeared to Ivanka and Mirjana.

Mirjana was asked, "If you knew the forthcoming sequence of events and had no faith, how would you live through this waiting period?"

"I would go crazy," she replied.

"But you have your faith."

"Yes, I am serene."

It would appear that hard times are coming to the world, and they are coming in the form of Divine retribution for the sins of mankind. If, however, we have responded to the messages of the Blessed Virgin Mary at Medjugorje, we don't have to worry. We will be in God's hands, and nothing can frighten us.

Sometimes I find people worried about the coming chastisements. I don't much like that word, but that's the word that the Visionaries have used. The Croatian word for chastisement can also be translated as "punishment" or "retribution." It is important to be aware that God is not a harsh, vengeful, angry Father. But there is no question that mankind has strayed from His protection. Has the world indeed brought this upon itself? All we have to do is read the papers. The Church is also having troubles. At no time in history have there been so many Christians dying for their faith. Martyrs are the story of the Church, and they come only when there is serious trouble. One does not have to hear about Medjugorje to know that people are starving to death, that there is corruption in high places, that abortion is a problem. Apparently things are going to get worse. So, what should we do? Put yourself in the Lord's hands. Take all this as a call to be converted and be closer to God. Pray that whatever disasters are coming might be mitigated, and that there might be some measure of peace in the world.

I think the main message of Medjugorje is the fact that the Blessed Virgin Mary is appearing so frequently—and not just for the parish or the young people, but for all the people in the world.

What does it all mean? At this time in history, through the providence of God, Mary is the mother of us all. She is my mother, and she is your mother. Jesus ratified that, when from the Cross He said to John: "Son (children), behold your mother." And to Mary: "Mother, behold your child." St John the Evangelist was standing in for each one of us—for me and for you.

Jesus first came to us through Mary, His mother. Now God has sent Jesus' mother to warn all the people of the earth to turn back to Him. Mary, His mother and ours, is calling us to be God's beloved, protected, and redeemed children.

—*Robert Faricy, SJ*

Mirjana

Podbrdo (Apparition Hill)

1

Mirjana

Live the Messages—Now!

Of the six Visionaries, Mirjana Dragicevic was the first to stop seeing the Blessed Mother daily. On Christmas Day, 1982, she was entrusted with the tenth secret, and now the Blessed Mother appears to Mirjana only on her birthdays and in times of special need. Recently she has also been communicating to her on the second day of each month, to help Mirjana with the burden of the secrets, and to prepare her for their imminent fulfillment.

For it is Mirjana who, at the Blessed Mother's instruction, will reveal the secrets one at a time through Fr. Petar Ljubicic in Medjugorje. He, in turn, will share them with the world—three days in advance of the events they prophesy.

Recently the Blessed Mother came to her with a message so full of sorrow that Mirjana was visibly upset as she repeated it:

Dear Children, I have been with you nine years. . . to tell you that God, your Father, is the only way, truth, and life. . . to show you the way that you can reach eternal life. . . . Give good example to your children, and those who do not believe. You will not have happiness on this earth, neither will you come to Heaven, if you do not have a pure and humble heart, and if you do not fulfill the laws of God.

Tears came to Mirjana's eyes, as she related what she had been told next.

I am asking for your help to join me in praying for those who do not believe. You are helping me very little. You have little charity or love for your neighbors, and God gave you the love, and showed you how you should forgive and love others. For that reason, reconcile. And purify your souls by going to confession. Take your rosary and pray. Take all your sufferings patiently. You should remember how patiently Jesus suffered for you.

The Blessed Mother had ended on an urgent note: *Do not impose your faith on the unbelievers; show it to them with your example. And pray for them, my children, pray.*

Mirjana is a contradiction of sorts. She is the only one of the Visionaries who left Medjugorje to seek a higher education—which she did with the Blessed Mother's encouragement. But it was a difficult time for her. She found herself alone in the cosmopolitan city of Sarajevo, living among young people for whom God did not exist. She wore a cross—and was scorned for doing so. It tried her faith—and caused her to completely dedicate herself to God. Today, as she helps with the Medjugorje pilgrims, she feels a special burden for young people who have no goal or purpose and care only for worldly, temporary things.

Mirjana is a very private person—yet gracious and possessing a measure of intellectual poise. At the same time she is deeply sensitive to the perilous state of the world; her anguish is evident to anyone who spends time with her. So is her compassion for those who don't know God. Her greatest fondness is for children. When she is around them, her customary reserve vanishes, and she beams.

[Ed. note: The following material, drawn from three interviews, has been organized according to subject matter. As with all the Visionaries, the interviews were taped and transcribed. Because of the language barrier, the interviews were conducted through an interpreter. To minimize distortion and ensure that they were as close to the intent of the Visionaries as possible, the author returned to Medjugorje with the interviews in manuscript form in English. Mirjana, who had studied English at the university, undertook to read the manuscript herself. The other Visionaries listened to an interpreter read their interviews in Croatian, for their approval. Fr. Tomislav Pervan, pastor of St James, Medjugorje, when the interviews began, subsequently scrutinized the manuscript.]

* * *

Mirjana, have you given many interviews since your daily apparitions stopped on Christmas day, 1982?
No, I give few interviews.
How often do you see the Blessed Mother now?
I see the Blessed Mother every year on my birthday, March 18, and she communicates with me by locution on the second of each month.

Can you describe what you mean by locution?

I "hear" the Blessed Mother, just as I hear you speak to me.

You hear her with your ears?

Yes.

Will you have this communication with the Blessed Mother for the rest of your life?

The Blessed Mother promised me something very special: she will appear to me every year of my life for my birthday and at moments when I have serious difficulty.

Does that mean, through you, the Blessed Mother will be appearing on the earth at least once a year for your entire life span?

Yes.

Do you know how long you will live?

No.

Is this the Blessed Mother's last apparition on earth?

The Blessed Mother said that.

What do you think that means?

The Blessed Mother has been here for a long time. You will understand when the secrets are fulfilled.

Can you give us a hint?

If you pray, you will know.

Will the Blessed Mother have messages for the world on your birthday each year?

Yes. Her messages on my birthday are for all her children in the world. I am just an instrument. At times of special difficulties in my life, the apparitions respond to the difficulties.

When you have these apparitions with the Blessed Mother, are you aware of being physically present during the apparition?

Yes. I am on the earth, with my body on the earth, touching the ground.

Are you fully conscious of where you are?
I'm not aware of anything except the presence of the Blessed Mother.
Could you describe how you felt when the apparitions began?
The first day, when Ivanka told me she saw the Blessed Mother, I didn't believe her. I was only fifteen. I felt the Blessed Mother was in Heaven. I didn't think she would bother with someone like us. I had never heard of Fatima or Lourdes. I didn't know anything about apparitions. When Ivanka told me to look at the mountain, I didn't bother to look. I wondered what was happening with her. We went back home, and later that evening, Milka Pavlovic asked Ivanka and me to help her round up some sheep. I wanted to go back to the mountain, and so we went with her. There was the Blessed Virgin Mary on the mountain where she had been before!
What was your reaction?
I was terrified! But the next day around the same time, we felt the desire to go to the same place, and then from the road we heard the Blessed Mother calling to us to come up to the hill.
You heard her?
Yes, and she waved to us. We were at the foot of the hill. She was calling us to come to her.
You weren't afraid anymore?
We were afraid! When we came to her the second day, we just fainted!
You fainted? Why?
Because I didn't understand anything, and I was seeing her, the Mother of God!
What did the apparition look like at this moment?
There was incredible light. The Blessed Mother

held the baby Jesus in her arms, covering and uncovering Him as she called to us. It was overwhelming! We are from a small village, not like young people from America or Europe. The girls here have never been anywhere away from home. Home, school, family—this is our life.

Who was the first to speak?

Ivanka.

What did she say?

She asked the Blessed Virgin Mary about her own mother who had died a month earlier. The Blessed Mother told her that her mother was in Heaven, that her mother was with her, and that she was well.

Did you hear the Blessed Mother say that?

Yes.

Then what happened?

The first few days we went back to the same spot and were still frightened. The first week the Blessed Mother did not speak a great deal. She was aware of our discomfort and was very loving. She was very, very kind to me. Then she began to tell us why she came.

Was that when the Blessed Mother began to speak about the secrets?

Yes. But when we shared what the Blessed Mother was saying, we had such persecution; nobody believed us! People said I had brought drugs from Sarajevo. I was fifteen years old; I hardly even knew about drugs then! People thought we were crazy.

What did the Blessed Mother say about all this?

The first time I heard what people were saying about me, I couldn't sleep all night long. But the next day the Blessed Mother told me that I shouldn't worry at all. I should never worry about anything that people would say about me. She told me everything would be okay.

And were you free from worrying?

Yes! I didn't worry any more at all. If people said I took drugs, I just laughed!

How powerful the Blessed Mother's effect on your soul was!

Yes, the Blessed Mother is the Queen of Peace. She always brings peace.

But things were far from peaceful in the beginning. The pastor, the mayor, the police, many of the villagers thought you were caught in a hoax. . . . How did your relationship with the Blessed Mother develop under such trying circumstances?

The Blessed Mother was very conscious of our fear. We talked, we prayed, and we sang. Gradually she led us to understand that she is our real mother. Later, as time went on and we began to be comfortable with her, we were able to speak to her as our mother about our problems and all our desires.

Why is the Blessed Virgin Mary our "real" mother?

Because she is the mother of our Eternal Life. She wants each of us—the children Jesus gave her from the Cross—in Heaven with Him, with God for all eternity.

What about our earthly mothers?

They give a child physical life when they bear that child. They lead a child to eternal life when they teach the child and raise the child in faith.

What should earthly mothers do?

They, along with the child's father, should consecrate all their children to God and teach their children to live a holy life.

Did the Blessed Mother ever physically touch you?
No.
Did you ever touch her?
Not me. Once I did see Jacov touch her. He was the youngest, just ten. We were all kneeling down, and the Blessed Mother appeared to us. It was August 5th, which the Blessed Mother had told us was her birthday. Jacov was very excited. As soon as she appeared, he reached out to touch her, and exclaimed, "Happy Birthday Holy Mother!" We were startled at his action. Embarrassed, he asked the Blessed Mother not to tell anyone what he had done.
What did the Blessed Mother do?
She took his hand and held it tenderly in hers.

[At the time of the author's first interview with Mirjana, she was still an undergraduate at the University of Sarajevo, studying economics.]
Mirjana, how much longer will you be a student?
I have four more exams, and then I will be finished.
Is the work hard?
Every day I think about being finished.
Do you pray about your school work?
Yes. Especially at exam time.
Do your prayers help you to get good grades?
Sometimes, when my grades are not very good, I ask my Jesus why He does not help me more.
Does He respond to you?
No. I know I am not successful, because I haven't studied enough.
During the time you were having daily apparitions with

the Blessed Mother, did she let you know whether she was interested in your schooling?

Yes. When the apparitions started, everybody thought we were crazy. The Blessed Mother told me that she would be happy if I would move away from Medjugorje and study something. She told me I was capable, and that she would like me to go to school.

The Blessed Mother told you to move away from here and go to school?

She did not tell me that I must; she said that she would be happy if I would. She wished me to go to school.

Did the Blessed Mother give you any other advice concerning your life?

Yes, she gave me a great deal of advice about how to live.

Would you share some of that?

For example, when we asked her what she would like us to do with the rest of our lives, she told us that if we choose to become nuns or priests, then we must be real nuns and priests. If we decide to get married and have a family, we should be an example of a good Catholic family to the world.

To the world?

Yes. These days it is most important for us to be examples to others of what family life should be.

Have you decided to get married, enter the convent, or remain single?

Not yet. I want to finish school first.

During your yearly apparition and the special communications you have with the Blessed Mother now, does she advise you about your life?

In the beginning she did. But now we spend most

of our time together praying for unbelievers, and we talk about the messages.

Does she tell you things to share with the world?

We six visionaries are not important. We are just like a telephone line for whatever God would like to say to the world. We are like a telephone line through which He communicates to His children.

Do you all receive the same messages?

The messages are the same for all of us, except for the secrets.

Mirjana, why has the Blessed Mother come?

She is our mother, and she would like all of us to heed the messages she is giving us. She wishes this so that later, when the secrets are to be revealed, there will not be any unbelievers.

Do you know whether all will believe when the signs begin?

There will still be unbelievers when the time comes for the secrets.

Many people ask whether the Blessed Mother's appearances here at Medjugorje mean that we have entered the End Times? Has the Blessed Mother said anything about the Apocalypse or the Second Coming of Christ?

That is part of the secrets. I would not like to talk about it.

Should we be frightened?

No, not at all. I've seen Heaven! Nothing of the earth is worth one moment of worry. We are God's children! If people only realized how much He loves us, and what He has prepared for us, they would be filled with such peace!

Mirjana, you are often quoted as saying that people who do not convert will have terrible suffering—is that true?

Yes. That is nothing new for Christians. God created

us for Himself, but He gave us free will. Those who use their freedom to choose things that are not of God will suffer the tortures of children of Satan. God gives His children Heaven, but Satan brings his children to Hell with him.

Has the Blessed Mother spoken about that?

Of course. That's why she has come.

Mirjana, you have been quoted as saying that you know not only the ten secrets, but also the different dates on which these secrets will come to pass. Is that true?

Yes.

Does this cause you suffering?

At first it caused me immense pain. But the Blessed Mother has helped me.

Can you tell us anything—?

There will be events on the earth as warnings to the world before the visible sign is given to humanity.

Will these happen in your lifetime?

I will be a witness to them.

In what way?

Three days before each of the events I will notify Fr. Petar Ljubicic.

What role do you play as an advance witness to these secrets?

My witness will be an affirmation to the world of the authenticity of the apparitions at Medjugorje and a stimulus for the conversion of the world.

Will many people die between the time of the first chastisement or event or admonition and the Permanent Sign promised at Medjugorje?

After the visible sign those still alive will have little time for conversion.

Mirjana, that makes God sound so cruel.

Oh no! God is not cruel! God is love, only love.

Cruelty and evil come from Satan. But with our free will we choose God or Satan every moment. Those who freely choose Satan, who disobey God's commandments, will perish.

You once said that the Blessed Mother explained to you that people in Hell do not pray. That they blame God for everything. They bring Hell into themselves and, in effect, become one with it. That they get used to conflict, disorder, utter lack of peace. They rage against God in a constant state of anger. They suffer, but they refuse to turn to God for help or relief. Why won't they pray?

They hate God.

Does the Blessed Mother speak about unbelievers on this earth who hate God, who blame Him for every bad thing?

Yes. That is why she is here. She is begging all people on earth to turn to God, to convert. She is the mother of all people on earth, and she does not want even one of her children in Hell.

What happens to people who refuse to convert, to turn back to God, to reconcile with one another?

They will suffer punishment, terrible punishment of their own choosing.

Does the Blessed Mother speak to you about that?

Yes. That is why she is crying. She is pleading with us to pray for the unbelievers so that they can realize the love God has for all His children. He loves what He creates.

What do you recommend we do?

Accept the deep peace and happiness that comes when we surrender to God and have been reconciled with our brothers and sisters. The Blessed Mother greatly desires that no one on earth be excluded from this peace and happiness.

How should we go about this?

Pray, especially during the Mass, and talk to unbelievers; encourage them to live the Blessed Mother's messages. There is much grace available for that right now. Most of all, ask believers to show by example what faith is.

Then we should speak about the Blessed Mother's messages to others?

Yes, but carefully. Do not go from house to house. If you have some friends whom you really care about and know are unbelievers, then out of love, talk to them. But slowly. You cannot push them, because they will only be able to understand a little at a time. Pray for them, and show them by your own example what the response to these messages is.

Do you have any practical advice to share that you, yourself, have learned from the Blessed Mother?

Yes: in every nice thing that you see on earth, recognize God. Be thankful to God. Remember Him every day. Talk to Him every day. Try to be aware of His immense love.

In a vision, Pope Leo XIII saw that Satan was given one century to test the Church—is this that century?

Yes. Many people have known this for a long time. Satan will rule until the first secret is unfolded.

Will the fulfillment of the secrets at Medjugorje break the power of Satan?

Yes.

How?

That is part of the secrets.

Concerning this century, is it true that the Blessed Mother related a dialogue to you between God and the devil? In it the devil claimed that people believed in God only when life was going well for them. The moment things turned bad, they ceased to believe in God. Then people blamed Him, or acted as if there was no God. And so God allowed the devil one century in which to exercise extended power, and the devil chose the 20th century.

Yes. Today, you can see Satan's power everywhere: everyone is dissatisfied; people cannot get along with each other. Divorce, broken marriages, abandoned children, born and unborn, grudges and bitterness within families, between brothers and sisters, parents and children, husband and wife—all this, the Blessed Mother said, is the handiwork of the devil.

All these things come from Satan?

Certainly. They come from sin. At least one person has to commit a sin for these acts to take place. He always tries to get people to sin. Wherever there is lack of love by someone, Satan is influencing that person.

In the modern world, many do not believe that Satan exists.

Oh, yes, he exists! I've had personal experience with him. Satan is the most evil force in creation. Encounters with him are horrible.

In Fr. Svet's book[1], you described waiting in your room for the Blessed Mother: "I knelt down and had not yet made the sign of the cross, when suddenly a bright light flashed and a devil appeared. . . . terrifying, dreadful, and I did not know what he wanted. I realized I was growing weak, and then I fainted. When I revived, he was still standing there, laughing. It seemed that he gave me a strange kind of strength so that I could almost accept him. He told me that I would be very beautiful and very happy and so on. However, I would have no need of the Madonna, he said, and no need for faith. 'She has brought you nothing but suffering and difficulties,' he said. But

he would give me everything beautiful, whatever I want.
Then something in me—I don't know what, if it was
something conscious or something in my soul—told me,
'No! No! No!' Then I began to shake and feel just awful.
Then he disappeared, and the Madonna appeared. When
she appeared, my strength returned—as if she restored it
to me. I felt normal again. Then the Madonna told me,
'That was a trial, but it will not happen to you again.' "
That experience was terrifying. I don't like to think
about it ever.

How do we recognize Satan's presence?
He always allures us by promising the beautiful
things of the world. He always tries to turn a true
believer away from the path to Heaven. Satan is evil
itself, but he always comes disguised. Usually, you can
sense his presence when there is confusion or
disorder or conflict. He particularly enjoys destroying
family relationships. He is very powerful. He can
distort memories; he can even distort what we think
is reality. He always wants to get us to sin. That is
why the Blessed Mother always calls us to live in peace,
to trust God and surrender to Him in everything. The
Blessed Mother says that to have this peace, we must
reconcile with one another in every situation. If we
forgive one another and truly love one another, Satan
loses his power. He has no place where there is love
and forgiveness.

Can you give us an example of his manipulation?
Yes. Sometimes when you are thinking about
praying or going to Mass or giving money to charity,
something will disturb you or interrupt you or distract
you. The phone will ring as you are about to leave
for church, or you will think of something else to
use your money for, to please yourself. That is Satan.

How can we recognize his influence?

By your own actions. When you find yourself doing something evil or something to hurt someone, you know he is involved with you.

What should we do?

Turn to God and ask His help.

Does the Blessed Mother tell us to do that?

Yes. She tells us to listen to Jesus, to be like Jesus.

Is it evil to get angry?

Yes. Anger is a big evil and a favorite tool of Satan.

Could you explain what you mean?

Well, for example, I have a brother who is fifteen years younger than I am. He is the youngest in the family, and often he feels like a baby. Sometimes he will ask me to cut his meat at the table. The thought comes into my head: "He is perfectly capable of cutting his own meat," and I experience feelings of anger. But the Blessed Mother told me that is Satan when I feel angry. If I shout at my little brother, then mother will shout at me, and father will shout at mother, and soon the whole family will be shouting at one another. The Blessed Mother has told me to pray in her name at those moments when I experience feelings of anger. I say, "Mary help me!" Then I can cut his pork chop and say, "Would you like me to cut some more?" So many things we do Satan influences, and we aren't even aware of it. He particularly affects our feelings. We need to pray about our feelings.

Speaking of feelings, you once mentioned the Blessed Mother coming in tears.

Yes. The Blessed Mother is often crying because of the sinful ways into which we have fallen. She says God's heart is full of compassion. She is asking all of us to turn to God, to trust Him. She never raises her voice. She never says anything hurtful. And people have hurt her so much, especially with this apparition. They deny her presence, find fault with us, so many things. She is our Mother. She is crying because of the danger we are in when we distance ourselves from God, and she is always praying for us. She is pleading for us to pray.

To pray?

Yes. It is through prayer that we experience God's love for us. And we should learn from her warning about Satan: if someone shouts—in a family, or at work or school—then the other person will shout, and the third person will shout, and Satan will have influenced everyone. Everyone is angry. Everyone has sinned.

Is Satan behind the first shout?

I believe so, because Satan is always leading us to sin.

Why?

I ask myself that many times.

When you feel angry, does prayer always work for you?

The Blessed Mother taught me to think of her Son: no matter what the executioners did to Him during His passion, they could not lead Jesus to respond with the sin of anger.

How do you overcome Satan's temptations?

The Blessed Mother said we overcome Satan by prayer and fasting. We are God's children when we pray, and the evil one has no power over God's children. It is only possible to forgive and to truly love everyone when we pray and fast. Otherwise our hearts are too hard to forgive. Also, we need to use

Holy Water and wear blessed objects. The most important thing we can do is to be truly vigilant in prayer.

How much do you pray?

Three rosaries a day.

How long does that take?

Several hours.

Do you have a special place where you pray?

Yes, in my room.

Do you go to Mass every day?

No. I am at the university all day, and there is no Mass there. But even if there was, I wouldn't go to church because I had to. I do go to Mass several times a week, because I feel God, my Father, calling me. He knows my circumstances. I always find a way to go to Mass when He calls me.

Do you have a favorite prayer?

Yes, the Hail Holy Queen[2].

Do you know the future of your life?

No. And I do not ask.

Have you seen Heaven, Hell or Purgatory?

I have seen Purgatory and Heaven, but I have not seen Hell because I did not want to see it.

Could you describe Heaven?

I saw Heaven as if it were a movie. The first thing I noticed was the faces of the people there; they were radiating a type of inner light which showed how immensely happy they were.

Is Heaven an actual place?

Yes. The trees, the meadows, the sky are totally different from anything we know on the earth. And the light is much more brilliant. Heaven is beautiful beyond any possible comparison with anything I know of on the earth.

Did the people you saw have bodies?
Yes.
What ages were they?
They were different from what we are like now.
Perhaps they were all around 30 years of age.
What were they doing?
They were walking in a beautiful park. They have
everything. They need or want nothing. They are
totally full.
What were they wearing?
They were dressed in the types of clothing that
Jesus wore.
Did the men have beards?
I don't know. I was so excited that I don't remember
now.
Did these people see you?
I just saw them. It was a vision. It did not last very
long.
Mirjana, did you see Purgatory?
Yes. There are several levels in Purgatory. The more
you pray on earth, the higher your level in Purgatory
will be.
How many levels are there?
The lowest level is the closest to Hell, where the
suffering is the most intense. The highest level is
closest to Heaven, and there the suffering is the least.
What level you are on depends on the state of purity
of your soul. The lower the people are in Purgatory
and the less they are able to pray, the more they
suffer. The higher a person is in Purgatory and the
easier it is for him to pray, the more he enjoys praying,
and the less he suffers.
How long do people stay in Purgatory?
I don't know. I do know that the Blessed Mother

has asked us to pray for the souls in Purgatory. They are helpless to pray for themselves. Through prayer, we on earth can do much to help them. The Blessed Mother told me that when souls leave Purgatory and go to Heaven, most go on Christmas day.

Mirjana, what, if anything, are you permitted to tell us about the ten secrets?

The first two secrets come as advance warnings for the whole world and as proof that the Blessed Mother is here in Medjugorje.

And the third secret?

The third secret will be a visible sign at Medjugorje—permanent, indestructible, and beautiful.

Are the ten secrets regional or global?

I may not answer that question.

Are they painful for Medjugorje or for the whole world?

The whole world.

You have said that the eighth secret is worse than the previous seven, and that the ninth is even worse, and the tenth is totally bad and cannot be lessened whatsoever— is that true?

I cannot say anything about that, because even a

word would disclose the secret before it's time to do so.

What should we do?

The Blessed Mother's messages here, prepare us for what is to come. She calls us to conversion now which means complete surrender to God. If we do that, we are not afraid, not even of death.

You said that the power of Satan would be broken by the fulfillment of the secrets—how?

I do not wish to comment further on the secrets.

It must have been quite painful for you, when the Blessed Mother stopped appearing daily to you.

I was so devastated that I wanted to die. I prayed and prayed, but the Blessed Mother did not appear. Finally, after six days she did appear, to explain to me that she would no longer be coming regularly, but only on my birthday, March 18th, and at times of grave difficulty. I didn't really believe this; I thought the apparitions would continue. I wanted them to so badly that I prayed and prayed. But the Blessed Mother said I had to live in the world like other people, without her daily presence. I was so sad at first that I was willing to die and be taken to Heaven, just to be with the Blessed Mother again.

Did you continue to hear the Blessed Mother with your ears?

No, but whenever I prayed, I could feel her close to me. And gradually, with her help, I came to accept things the way they are.

But now she is coming to you on the second of each month—can you tell us why?

The Blessed Mother comes to me now when I especially need her. And it is always concerning the secrets. Sometimes I hardly can stand the pressure of knowing them. During those moments the Blessed Mother comforts me and encourages me.

Are they that awful?

Yes, it is so hard for me. But as bad as they are, at the same time she had told me we should not be afraid. God is our Father, Mary is our Mother.

Then why are you so upset now, that the Blessed Mother must come to comfort and encourage you?

Because there are many who do not believe, who do not accept God as their Father, Mary as their Mother. I feel such sorrow for them that I can hardly bear it! My suffering is so great for them that I really must have the Blessed Mother's help to survive.

Your "suffering" is really compassion for the unbelievers?

Yes. They do not realize what awaits them!

How does the Blessed Mother console you?

She and I pray together for those who do not believe.

Who are these unbelievers?

Unbelievers are those who do not feel like going to the house of God the Father, the church. They even go to church merely out of habit. They have no desire for God, no ability to worship. They are spending their lives on things that pass away. Dissatisfaction, lack of peace, and sorrow are the real fruits of the labor of the unbeliever. The Blessed Mother is our mother. She feels great sorrow for her children's suffering when they waste their lives on things they can't keep. This is a time of great grace— but unbelievers are choosing to walk a path that leads nowhere.

Do the prayers that the Blessed Mother and you say together make a difference?

Well, I asked, and they do. And we pray to God, that He will change the hearts of unbelievers so that they, too, can have a desire for Him in their hearts.

Is that why the Blessed Mother asks all her faithful children in the world to pray now and fast and do penance?

Yes. She recommends that all of us pray—and as we pray, she will pray with us.

You have been with her now for more than nine years!

Yes, I have a very intimate mother/daughter relationship with her, based on her immense love for me. She, the mother of Jesus, would like to have this same relationship with every person on earth.

When you are not praying, what do you speak about?

We always speak about the rest of Mary's children, the needs of all her children. The Blessed Mother worries most of all about unbelievers. They will be left out.

What can we do?

The Blessed Mother would like all families to pray the rosary together. She pleads for a return to family prayer and longs for all God's children to want heaven. Nothing is important in the world now but prayer!

Is there any particular prayer?

Pray especially the rosary. The Blessed Mother says we have no idea how powerful the rosary is. When we pray it with our heart, contemplating each of the joyful, sorrowful and glorious mysteries of Jesus' life on earth, we walk beside Mary through His whole life. Jesus is the way to Heaven, whether people know Him by name or not. Those who walk with Mary on the path of Jesus' life, have life with God.

Mirjana, before we end, do you have any special advice?

Yes. Warn the people about Satan's power. He wants to steal Heaven from us. Tell them to pray and fast. Tell them of God's immense love for us. Tell them nothing of the earth has value unless it leads us to God. Tell them our true home is Heaven. No suffering on earth is too much when the true reward is Heaven. I've seen Heaven! It is such a gift of God's love! We are God's children; nothing of this earth is worth one moment of worry.

What must we do to gain Heaven?

Be a babe in God's arms.

At the cross on Podbrdo.

Two milk cows.

To the north, Mt Krizevac (Cross Mountain).

Ivanka and Kristina (held by author).

2

Ivanka

The Blessed Mother is always with us

Ivanka Ivankovic is the other Visionary who no longer sees the Blessed Mother every day. On May 6, 1985, two weeks after her nineteenth birthday, Ivanka received the tenth secret, at which time the Blessed Mother promised to appear to her every year on the anniversary of the apparitions. In December of the following year, Ivanka married Rajko Elez, and in November of '87, she and her husband had a baby daughter, Kristina, who was present at the first interview.

That interview was more like a social visit. Ivanka was holding her baby in her lap, and at one point, to illustrate her relationship with the Blessed Mother, she put her hands over Kristina's eyes. "Just because the baby doesn't see the mother," she said with a shy giggle, "doesn't mean the mother doesn't see the baby!"

She added that to know our mother Mary, we must open our hearts. Through faith we may accept her as our loving, caring mother, always with us. [At which point—this was the author's first interview with a

Visionary—she remembered to start her tape recorder. There would be four more meetings with Ivanka, the most recent taking place on August 5, 1989. At the end of it, Ivanka asked that the distillation of her previous interviews which had just been read to her in Croatian, be disseminated as widely and quickly as possible.]

Ivanka is an uncomplicated, unassuming young woman, not given to making a fuss over herself or probing into the details of her role. She seems content to let the messages speak for themselves, and does her best to live in obedience to them. The tallest of the Visionaries, she is quiet and hard-working, shy yet sensitive to the feelings of others. She possesses an underlying tranquility—and a gentle sense of humor occasionally bubbles up.

* * *

Ivanka, why is the Blessed Mother here?
Mary is the mother of Jesus. She is here in Medjugorje calling all people in the world to the path Jesus showed us. That path is the road to Heaven.
What must we do?
Pray. Always do good things for other people. The Blessed Mother has asked us to live her messages of peace, prayer, penance, fasting, conversion and reconciliation.
Ivanka, what does the Blessed Mother look like?
She is extremely beautiful. The Blessed Mother always comes with angels. There is always a great light before she comes.
Do the angels have bodies?
Yes, like babies. You can touch them.

Have you ever touched them?
Yes. I love them very much.
Are they on either side of the Blessed Mother?
They are above her.
When you hold little Kristina in your arms, do you think of the angels?
Yes. I pray to them every day.
Is the Blessed Mother dressed differently every time she comes?
Not every time. But for Christmas she wore a golden dress. At the sleeves and hem of the dress were golden circles.
Was the dress itself gold?
The dress was luminescent with gold coming from it.
Is the Blessed Mother sad sometimes?
Yes.
Why?
She is praying for us and hoping to lead us to conversion. Not everyone in the world is paying attention.
Does it hurt the Blessed Mother when we sin?
Yes. Because she knows how much the sin hurts us. She loves us so much that her pain is very great, when she sees how our sins hurt us.
So the Blessed Mother really cares about us?
Yes. I know she loves every person on the earth. We are all her children.
How do you know that she loves all of us?
Because I myself have experienced her love. I know from my years with the Blessed Virgin Mary how very much she, as our mother, loves each one of us.
Why is she concerned with everyone in the world?
The Blessed Mother is our mother. She doesn't

want to be denied the presence of any one of her children for eternity. She wants all of her children to be with her Son, Jesus. She wants all of her children to have the happiness of Heaven.

Do you think about the Blessed Mother all the time?
Yes, she has shown me God's Kingdom.
Does God love everybody in the world, even though they sin?
He loves everybody. We are all His children. He sent Jesus to redeem us from our sin. God forgives any sinner who asks for forgiveness.

Did you see Heaven, Hell and Purgatory, Ivanka?
I saw Purgatory and Heaven as a picture. I told the Blessed Mother I did not want to see Hell.
What did Heaven look like?
It is a place that is very, very beautiful. Most beautiful.
Were there houses in Heaven?
None that I saw.
Were there trees?
No, I saw only people.
Did they have bodies?
Yes, they did.
What did they wear?
I saw them in gray robes.
Were they happy?
Everyone I saw was filled with a happiness I can't explain—and I can't forget!
Do you long for that happiness yourself?
I know some of that happiness when I am with the Blessed Mother, and when I pray.

Did everyone wear gray clothes?

Yes, but the clothes didn't matter. They were not a part of the happiness.

Can you tell us more about Heaven?

God made us for Heaven. If you pray, you will know that.

What was Purgatory like?

Only darkness.

Did you think you were dreaming when you saw these things?

No. I saw these places as in a picture.

Why did the Blessed Mother show you Heaven and Purgatory?

She wants to remind her children of the results of their choices here on earth.

Ivanka, are we ever a good judge of our own holiness?

No. We are never a good judge of anything. God is the only judge. Only God knows our heart.

Does God love unbelievers, too?

God loves everybody in the whole world. He made everyone. He loves everyone.

What does that mean?

God is the Creator. He loves what He creates.

How do we love Him back?

We love God through prayer. We love God through love. Those who are helping others are loving others just like God loves us. Sometimes there are better people who think they do not believe, than people who say they do believe. Many believers do not pray. The more we pray, the closer we come to God.

How do we know God's will, Ivanka?

By prayer.

What about people who don't pray?

People know whether they are living in God's will or not by how much peace they have. If they don't feel peace in their hearts, they know they are not doing the right thing. Those who are doing God's will have peace. Their life is filled with joy and contentment, even in the midst of the worst sorrow.

So the test for whether we are doing the right thing on earth or not is how much peace we feel?

That's right.

Ivanka, can you tell us about seeing your mother?

Yes. In the early days of the apparitions, my mother whom I had been close to, had suddenly died. I was very lonely for her. I asked the Blessed Mother if she knew about my mother. The Blessed Mother told me, yes, my mother was with her.

Oh, Ivanka, that must have made you happy!

It made me very happy!

Did you ask the Blessed Mother about your mother?

I asked her if I could see my mother.

Did she permit you to?

I've seen my mother three times since she died!

Can you tell us what she looked like?

My favorite time was the last time she was with the Blessed Mother. My mother came over to me. She put her arms around me and kissed me. She said, "Oh, Ivanka, I am so proud of you."

Was it different than the kisses your mother gave you before she died?

No. It was the same.

Ivanka, did your mother look the same?

Yes, just the same.

Her hair was the same? Her face—the same wrinkles, the same smile, the same look?

Yes. The same. Everything was the same.

Was she dressed the same way as on earth?

Oh, no. She wore a long gray robe.

Ivanka, how extraordinary! When we drive away from your house today, we will pass the cemetery where your mother is buried. And yet, you saw her in her body just as if she were still on earth. Yet she was dead. Did seeing her give you joy?

Oh, yes. Great joy.

Has it made a difference in your life?

Now I know what the "Communion of Saints" which we mention each day in the Creed means, through personal experience.

Do you know other things, too?

Yes. The Blessed Mother's gifts to me have been great. I know there is a Heaven, because I have seen it. I know my mother is in Heaven, because I have personally seen her three times since she has died. I know that if I obey God's will, and I am faithful to God, I will be in Heaven, too.

Do you long for Heaven, Ivanka?

I long for God.

Did you always long for God, Ivanka?

The Blessed Mother taught me how to pray. She brought me to God.

Ivanka, is it true that this is the Blessed Mother's last apparition on earth?

Yes, it is.

Ivanka, you see the Blessed Mother each year on the anniversary of the apparitions—can you describe your apparition of June 25, 1988?

Yes. The Blessed Mother was very beautiful. She had gold around the edges of her dress and her veil this time. She spoke to me particularly about the third and fourth secrets.

Is there anything you can share with us?

No.

Is there anything in the secrets that should frighten us?

No. Nothing should frighten us except disobeying God's will.

Can you tell us about your apparition of June 25, 1989?

Yes. We spoke about the 5th and 6th secrets.

How did the Blessed Mother look?

She was extremely beautiful. Again, she had gold around the edges of her dress and veil.

What else did Blessed Mother speak about?

The Blessed Mother wants us to pray much more, because Satan wants to take over our lives. He is doing everything he can and is using every advantage to do this, especially in our material lives. Blessed Mother wants us to continue to pray and fast. She is interceding to her Son for us.

Did the Blessed Mother give you anything else you can share with us?

The Blessed Mother wants everyone in the world to live the messages, especially to pray and fast.

Why should we fast?

We should fast for the sake of greater freedom. Fasting will free us from things. The Blessed Mother has said that praying and fasting can even stop wars.

Will there be war?

Praying and fasting can stop war.

Fasting will give us greater freedom—how?

It will give us freedom to serve God and the Blessed Mother and our brothers and sisters, when we don't worry about our own needs and wants all the time.

Can you tell me how you fast?

On Wednesdays and Fridays, I fast on bread and water.

What do you do during Lent?

During Lent I fast on bread and water for forty days, just like my relatives have done for 700 years. I started doing this because the Blessed Mother told me that fasting will stop wars. I know the future of the world—not just my own life history but the future of the world.

Tell me about this knowledge you have concerning the future of the world?

It is a heavy burden. I know I must pray and fast as the Blessed Mother asked.

How do you manage with such a heavy burden?

I simply go ahead and live my own life. I don't think about it all the time. Anytime I think about it, I try to pray more and fast.

When you pray and fast, do you have peace?

Yes. The Blessed Mother told us never to focus on bad things. She told us always to focus on God—on His love for us, and on the future He has planned for us in Heaven.

Ivanka, are we pilgrims an imposition?

No, not at all. The Blessed Mother told me people would be coming from all around the world. She asked us to welcome them in our homes the way we would like to be welcomed. She reminded us that when she and Joseph went to Bethlehem when the baby Jesus was born, no one had room for them. We are always happy to have the pilgrims come, because they love God so much, they love the Blessed Mother so much. And they are coming here seeking freedom. They are coming here seeking truth. They are coming here seeking God.

Ivanka, what do you do when you are very tired, when you seem to have more work to do than you can accomplish in a day's time?

I always pray, and I never feel that way. When I pray, I feel much peace.

Where is your favorite place to pray?

At Mass. The Mass is the center of my life.

Why?

The Blessed Mother taught me the value of the Mass.

Do you have any other special places you like to pray?

Yes. I like to climb the mountain and pray.

Do you pray as a family?

Yes. My husband and I and his family pray the rosary together every day.

Does that seem to make a difference in your life?

We are obeying the Blessed Mother. She asked us to pray as a family. She told me that families who pray together have peace.

What happens to families who do not pray together?

The Blessed Mother said that prayer can stop war.

If families don't pray, can they expect to have a war in the family?

The Blessed Mother promised that if families pray together, they will have peace in their families.

Do you have much suffering?

My main suffering involves the secrets.

What did the Blessed Mother tell you about suffering?

The Blessed Mother has told me about the future of the world. For over two years she talked about the future. She talks to each of us visionaries differently. To me she talks about the future of the world. To Vicka she speaks about her own life.

What did the Blessed Mother tell you? Is it a good future?

The Blessed Mother has told me everything. There are good things and bad things. The important thing is to know that God loves each of us. We are all His children.

Is it a long future?

For some it is long; for some it is short.

Ivanka, I hesitate to ask this, but I feel I must: would God destroy this world?

We are destroying this world, not God.

Is the destruction of the world part of the secrets?

I may not speak about the secrets.

Do you worry much about them?

When the Blessed Mother comes to me each year, she talks to me about the secrets. She shares things with me.

Later on, when the secrets come to pass, will you have a role to play in the unfolding of them?

We will all have a role to play in the unfolding of the secrets. That is part of God's plan.

Part of God's plan? What do you mean?

Each person on the earth will be involved in the unfolding of the secrets. God calls us all to be faithful, in all circumstances of our lives. He calls us to be faithful to His will. Through prayer, each of us knows what that is.

In light of your knowledge of all ten secrets, what would you recommend?

Pray. Always pray. Try to do good things for other people. Try to live the messages. Please ask people to take them seriously. Please accept God's great gift to us. Please do what the Blessed Mother asks of you. Then you will have great peace and joy on this earth, even in suffering. You will have Heaven for all eternity.

To the south, snow-capped Mt Belez.

Early on a frosty morning. . . .

Next to the rectory,
towering shade.

Vicka

3
Vicka

Pray for the lost souls!

[Of all the Visionaries, the author spent the most time with Vicka. From January of '88 to March of '90, she met with her on six separate occasions, each time at considerable length in her room and always at the Visionary's invitation.]

Anyone meeting Vicka Ivankovic for the first time is instantly taken with her radiant smile. It is a smile that does not leave her, although her life is given from sun-up to sun-down to meeting with one group of pilgrims after another. Often they are lined up in the narrow street outside her house, awaiting their turn—a group from Italy behind a group from Ireland behind one from the Philippines. . . .

What is the Blessed Mother wearing? What is her hair like? Do you actually hear her? During the past nine years Vicka must have heard the identical questions thousands of times, yet always she answers with enthusiasm and patience, as if she had never heard it before.

Of medium height with dark, curly hair and flashing

dark eyes, Vicka is forthright and direct; she says exactly what she thinks. Nor is she easily impressed; for her, life with God is the only thing that matters. Her vibrant effervescence has been tempered somewhat by the severity of the physical suffering she has endured; she is more pensive now, and surrendered. Her life is totally committed to imparting the messages, and to sharing her experience with any who will listen. Sometimes, after dark, she will slip up Podbrdo behind her house and pray—alone or with a few friends. That is her only respite. The rest of her life is poured out in selfless service. Perhaps for this reason she is the Visionary to whom the Blessed Mother has confided the details of her life.

In 1986, Vicka, suffering from increasingly painful headaches, was diagnosed as having an inoperable brain tumor and swelling of the joints which eventually resulted in high fevers and comas. On February 25, 1988, the Blessed Virgin Mary instructed Vicka to write three letters: to Father Janko Bubalo, her confessor; to the Bishop's Commission investigating the Apparitions; and to the priests in residence at the Rectory of St James, Medjugorje. These letters were sealed and delivered to the above-named persons. On September 25, 1988 (two months and three weeks after her 24th birthday), Vicka asked the recipients of the sealed letters to open them in the presence of two witnesses. Each of the letters written seven months before, contained the same information: Vicka's illness was God's gift to her, not a punishment. It was accepted voluntarily, and its purpose was to help heal the illness of sinners. Her sacrifice would be completed on September 25; on that date she would be healed of her illness. And she was.

Anyone tempted to envy Vicka's role need only observe her for a day. She has no life of her own. Nor does she want one. Her only desire is to help save the lost, and for this she gladly pours herself out endlessly. Why does she care so much? The following interview will make that obvious.

* * *

Vicka, why is the Blessed Mother appearing in Medjugorje?

She wants everyone in the whole world to be saved, to live in God's loving presence. She has come to call all people in the world to listen to her messages and convert. It is dangerous to live in sin. Terrible catastrophes await those who do not turn back to God. But He always forgives us, no matter what the sin. All we have to do is ask. The Blessed Mother is calling us to ask His forgiveness now. She reminds us that God never refuses forgiveness to any of His children who ask.

There are millions of people on earth who are not Christian—what does the Blessed Mother want of them?

To pray. All people on earth are born with a knowledge of God in their hearts. Everyone has his own way to pray. The Blessed Mother is the mother of all people on earth. She has a mother's love for them all, and her messages, which are from God, are for everyone.

Then it doesn't matter what name or person they call God?

There is only one God. It is man who makes divisions.[1] Jesus came for all people on earth, whether they know it or not.

What role does Mary play?

Mary, the mother of all, brings her children to her Son who takes them to the Father.

How long have you been seeing the Blessed Virgin Mary and hearing this profound message?

Since June 24, 1981.

When she comes, do you immediately feel her holiness?

Absolutely. You can feel it very powerfully.

Can you describe what happens?

When the Blessed Mother comes, she is always preceded by a brilliant light. First, she greets me. Then she says some special or personal things, and we pray together. Sometimes she blesses everybody who is here. Sometimes she prays for those who are ill.

What does she look like?

She has blue eyes, very beautiful eyes. And her hair is black and long and has some curl. She wears a long shimmering dress and a veil, and around her head there are always twelve stars, like a crown.[2]

What color is her dress?

It's a different color than we are used to seeing on earth. It seems to me that the closest color I could name would be gray, but it's not really gray the way we know gray. Her veil is a glowing white.

Is she always dressed the same way?

No. For special Feasts the Blessed Mother sometimes wears dresses that are of gold, and her veil is of gold, and she has many jewels.

What message does she bring on such days?

The Blessed Mother always says peace must reign between God and man and also among men.

Have you ever seen her wear any other color?

Yes. Depending on the Feast, she has worn dresses

of turquoise and many other shades that are most beautiful.

Have you ever seen her shoes?

No. I have never seen the Blessed Mother's feet. I have never seen her walk.

How does she arrive and depart?

She appears in a radiant light and disappears as the light fades.

Is the Blessed Mother tall?

A bit taller than I am. She is about the height of Ivanka.

Does she look anything like the photographs you have seen?

I have never seen any painting or statue or picture that looks like the Blessed Mother.

Is she beautiful?

The Blessed Mother has a beauty that is unlike anything on earth. When she smiles, I feel such joy! Her beauty and presence are beyond my ability to describe! And when she is gone, I feel a great loneliness. But when I see that smile, that radiance— I feel I must be in Heaven!

What do you think of when you do try to describe her?

Pure love.

Before your first apparition, when you were sixteen, had you ever heard of Fatima, or Lourdes or any other apparitions of the Blessed Mother?

No.

What happened the first time you saw her?

I was so frightened that I ran away. I ran so fast, I left my sandals behind.

And then, the next day?

God's grace was stronger.

And each day was it better?

Yes.

Is the Blessed Mother happy when you see her?

Sometimes she is sad; sometimes she is crying, because people don't always obey God, and they have no idea how much their sin hurts them.

Has she ever been angry?

Oh no! I've never seen the Blessed Mother angry! She is not like us. The Blessed Mother has only love and concern for us. How understanding and patient and caring the Blessed Virgin Mary is! She always gives us peace and tells us to have courage.

Is the apparition that of a real person, or is it more a mist-like vision?

The Blessed Mother is a real person. She has a real body, a real personality. I experience her as my mother. I am a child with my mother, when I am with the Blessed Virgin Mary. This relationship is not just for me: she has explained to me that she is the mother of each person in the whole world. She loves each of us as her own dear child. And she is calling us all to come back to God. The way is faith, peace, prayer, fasting, and conversion. But I want to say strongly: she is not distant, not far away from any of us on this earth! The Blessed Mother is very much a part of our life on the earth, very close to us, and very concerned about each one of us on the earth!

Vicka, you speak of her as if she was right here!

She is! If you pray with your heart, you, too, will be able to experience her presence.

I will?

The Blessed Mother has said that if we pray with our hearts, this experience of her presence, as well

as the presence of God in our life, is possible.
Do you have this experience continuously?
Yes. I always see the Blessed Mother with my heart.
During the time the Blessed Mother appears to me,
I see her with my eyes. The rest of the time I
experience her presence through prayer with the
heart.
Is she with everyone in the whole world?
Yes, of course. Most people on the earth do not
see her with their eyes, but they may see her with
their hearts. When I do not see her (sometimes she
has asked me to have weeks when I do not see her),
I see her with my heart, like everyone else.
Can everyone experience the Blessed Mother as you do?
Or is this apparition for you alone?
This apparition is for all people on earth! *It is time
for all people to know their heavenly mother.* If we open
our hearts to her, we may have a relationship with
her. If not, if we deny her presence in our life, she
is too humble to impose herself upon us. She always
invites us to life with God.
Why does she only 'invite' us?
She never commands. Only God commands.
The Blessed Mother sounds so loving.
Our relationship with the Blessed Mother depends
on whether we accept her presence in our lives and
open our hearts to her. She is always there for us.
We are free to reject her or to love her. It is up to
us. If we learn to pray with our hearts, all of us can
experience her presence with eyes of faith. That is
why she always asks us to "open our hearts." She
wants us to set aside all that is disturbing us. She
wants us to have a really joyful prayer life by coming
closer to her.

Is that what you mean by "surrender?"

Yes. Become aware by opening our "spiritual eyes" that God and the Blessed Mother are looking at us, that we always live in the presence of God, the Angels and the Saints.[3] She has said: *"Dear children, when you have problems, when you have troubles, when you think that Jesus and I are far away from you, we are always near you. You must open your hearts so you can recognize us with your hearts. Then you will be able to see how much we love you."* The more we open our hearts through prayer and fasting, the more we can understand and accept this.

How do you "open your heart," Vicka?

When I pray the Our Father, I think about what each phrase means—who He really is and where He is. It is something like our relationships with our fathers here on earth. If we hear them and see them all the time, then we know them. So, with prayer and deep thinking we can discover our Heavenly Father, just as we discovered and learned about and know our father on earth. Just think constantly on this: with prayer we can open our hearts to God.

Why are so many people unaware?

Where you live there are many who have weak faith. The Blessed Mother loves all her children, especially her weak children, her lost children. She prays and intercedes before God day and night for each of her children.

Her main message here is prayer, isn't it?

Yes, because it deepens our faith. When we pray, we begin to experience God in every little thing. We can hear Him and see Him. We can really have a relationship with Him. Prayer is the key to God.

You seem to live in the presence of God and the Blessed Mother all the time—is that difficult?

It takes faith!

Why has the Blessed Mother come at this time?

The Blessed Mother comes to us from God. She knows what God's will for us is. She knows the consequences to us, if we do not live in God's will.

How do you know God's will?

Through prayer.

Has the Blessed Mother spoken about this apparition being her last?

Yes, the Blessed Mother said that it is the last apparition ever.

Everybody is wondering why she is appearing for so long.

It is because everybody is her child. The Blessed Mother says: *"I love everybody as my own son and daughter, and I want everyone to be saved. I don't want a single one of my children in Hell."* She is hoping people will accept these messages little by little. And they are. She says praying the rosary, especially as a family, and fasting, are powerful ways to rescue souls for the kingdom of her Son. She recommends to us to pray all three mysteries of the rosary every day, the Joyful, Sorrowful and the Glorious. To fast on bread and water every Friday and if possible on Wednesdays, too. When she asks us to pray, she does not mean to pray with mere words; she wants us to pray with our hearts, so that prayer can become a wellspring of happiness to us. Then we will know of God's immense love, of His great mercy. He loves all His children. He forgives; He never turns anyone away, no matter what we have done.

Then why do people not turn to Him and ask forgiveness?

Lots of reasons. Satan can make people believe

they aren't worthy of forgiveness. Or, when our hearts are hard, we don't want forgiveness, and we won't forgive each other. Some people don't know God, because they don't pray. Some people think God is cruel. Man can be cruel, but God has only love for His poor, sinful children.

Even God's justice is kindness, for it cleanses.

That is why our Blessed Mother has come to Medjugorje. The messages she brings are a sign of God's great love for us. She is calling us to conversion *now.*

Is it important that the world become aware of the Blessed Mother's messages?

It is urgent that everyone become aware now. Take the messages to your friends and relatives, but more than that: to everyone in the whole world who will listen. The Blessed Mother wants these messages known by all people on earth. She wants each one who hears them to *live* them and by their own lives be an example of God's great love for His redeemed children. Ask those who hear them to tell others, to share, to help the Blessed Mother.

Is that why you speak to so many people all day long?

Yes. This is what the Blessed Mother wants from me. God chose me.

Isn't it hard?

It is a great gift for me. But it is also. . . sometimes. . . . I'm trying with love. . . . I want to bring the Blessed Mother closer to everyone in the world. She loves us, and she is worried about us because so many people just ignore God.

Would you like to emphasize any part of the messages?

In these last days the Blessed Mother is urging us to pray, especially for youth all over the world, because they are having great difficulties. And we are the only ones able to help them, by prayer and love coming from our hearts. The Blessed Mother said: *"Dear children, this is a grave period of great seriousness; I long for you to start living these messages with your whole heart."* She asks us to be the carrier of her peace, and to pray for peace in the world.

Vicka, if we don't pray for peace, will there be war?

First, we must pray for peace in our own hearts, then in our families, and only then in the whole world.

If one person in the family prays, will all the family be saved?

So it is; our prayers are never useless.

In families where some will not pray and believe, should the loved ones just pray for them and have faith? Will the unbelieving family members come back to God?

Yes. Our words cannot help, only prayers and sacrifices.

So prayer is the most powerful weapon?

Yes. Especially the prayer of the rosary.

You keep emphasizing the rosary. What about non-Catholics?

They must pray in their own way, of their own faith. We are all God's children. It isn't God who makes differences on earth, but people themselves. Anyway, all are invited to pray the rosary. It is for everyone in the world, not just Catholics.

How should we pray?

We have to feel the prayer as something living in our hearts, so that possibly we can only pray ten Hail Mary's the whole day and nothing else. And the day after, you can go on with ten other prayers. The Blessed Mother has said that sometimes you will love praying the whole rosary, and you pray and you pray.

On other days you will feel nothing, and you're not satisfied; it is as if you didn't pray at all. But our feelings are not the reason we pray; we pray because God has called us to pray.

How has the Blessed Mother taught you to pray?

The best way is to fall on our knees and place ourselves before the cross, in our hearts. In this moment we talk to Jesus, because we are together. We present our desires, our problems to Him, asking His help to give away all these thoughts, so that our hearts can be pure to pray with Him. We begin to experience through Christ that we truly have a loving Father. So we open ourselves to be able to love Him also. When these two loves come together, that is real prayer!

You look as if you have great joy in prayer.

I do! When you pray with your heart, there is great satisfaction in prayer.

How sad for those who don't know that!

It is sad that all do not have this joy in prayer. But in our communication with God, we can pray in a way that some part of this joy falls on these persons.

Is the important thing to live in God's love every moment, every day?

Exactly! Have great confidence in our loving God! Enjoy living in His presence. Our prayer life is not a duty. When we experience being in the presence of God even our work is a prayer. Everything is a prayer.

What can you tell us about prayer groups?

The Blessed Mother is happy to see any prayer groups; there is great power in group prayer. She would like the prayer groups to pray so that God's plan for the salvation of the world, being manifested here through the Blessed Mother, can be realized. We are to pray for that, and for all the people in the world, not just for our problems or friends. If we pray for God's plan here, He will reward us.

We really don't know how powerful prayer is, do we?

No. By prayer with the heart and by fasting, by taking bread and water on Wednesdays and Fridays, we can stop wars.

What kind of war?

Little wars, big wars—all wars.

Did one of the Blessed Mother's messages concern divorce?

Yes. She said that she was very sad about this. The number of divorced people there are in the world shows the power Satan has over people's lives.

Vicka, is it true that you yourself have personally seen Heaven, Hell and Purgatory?

Yes. The Blessed Mother has shown me Heaven, Hell, and Purgatory.

Why?

Many people today do not believe there is a place or state of life after death of the body. They believe that when we die, life is over. The Blessed Mother says no; on the contrary, we are only passengers on earth. She has come to remind us of the eternal truths of the Gospel.

Are Heaven and Hell actual places?

Yes. I saw them.

How?

Two ways—I saw with my eyes—

A vision?

Yes. And then I visited these places. Jacov and I were taken there by the Blessed Mother.

Vicka, tell us about Heaven.

Heaven is a vast space, and it has a brilliant light which does not leave it. It is a life which we do not know here on earth. We saw people dressed in gray, pink, and yellow robes. They were walking, praying, and singing. Small angels were flying above them. The Blessed Mother showed us how happy these people are.

How could you tell they were happy?

You can see it on their faces. But it is impossible to describe with words the great happiness I saw in Heaven.[4]

What a blessing that you have seen it!

Great rewards await those who are faithful!

Does the Blessed Mother meet everyone when they die and take them to Heaven?

Yes.

How do you know that?

In Paradise, when the Blessed Mother passed, everybody responded to her, and she to them. There was a recognition between them.

How? Did they show some sign, like Hello?

They were standing there communicating with her, like in a tunnel, only it wasn't exactly like a tunnel, but a tunnel is the closest comparison. People were praying, they were singing, they were looking.

Some people, when they heard what you said about everyone walking around Heaven singing and praying in pink, yellow and grey robes, said, "That sounds boring."

When God has filled you with His love, bored is a word that has no meaning. People in Heaven know the absolute fullness of a created being.

How long were you there?
Maybe twenty minutes.
Were you walking with those people?
Yes.
How were you dressed?
In my own dress.
Was there grass?
In some ways it was like this room, but mostly it was unlimited.
What did you walk on?
Well, it was like walking on the ground.
Were there any buildings?
None that I saw.
Did the people talk to you?
It was very unusual. They were speaking, but I could not understand them.
Did you inter-relate with them?
The people were in small groups. I was with Jacov and the Blessed Mother. We spoke to each other, but there was no communication with anyone else. About the people there, the Blessed Mother only said to us, "You see how people who are in Heaven are happy?"
Do you know whether there are relationships in Heaven— husband and wife, children, together?
We'll see.
What about Hell—is it a place, too?
Yes.
Do many people go there today?
Yes. We saw many people in Hell. Many are there already, and many more will go there when they die.
Why so many?
The Blessed Mother says that those people who are in Hell are there because they chose to go there. They wanted to go to Hell.

Vicka, why would anyone want to go there?

We all know that there are persons on this earth who simply don't admit that God exists, even though He helps them, gives them life and sun and rain and food. He always tries to nudge them onto the path of holiness. They just say they don't believe, and they deny Him. They deny Him, even when it is time to die. And they continue to deny Him, after they are dead. It is their choice. It is their will that they go to Hell. They choose Hell.

Describe Hell as you remember it.

In the center of this place is a great fire, like an ocean of raging flames. We could see people before they went into the fire, and then we could see them coming out of the fire. Before they go into the fire, they look like normal people. The more they are against God's will, the deeper they enter into the fire, and the deeper they go, the more they rage against Him. When they come out of the fire, they don't have human shape anymore; they are more like grotesque animals, but unlike anything on earth. It's as if they were never human beings before.

Can you describe them?

They were horrible. Ugly. Angry. And each was different; no two looked alike.

After they came out of the ocean of fire, what did they do?

When they came out, they were raging and smashing everything around and hissing and gnashing and screeching.

Were you afraid?

I am never afraid when I am with the Blessed Mother. But I didn't like seeing this. . . .

When you were there, could you feel the fire's heat?

No, we were in a special grace with the Blessed

Mother, so we felt nothing.

Vicka, you said that God condemns no one, that people choose Hell for themselves. Would it be fair, then, to say that if you can choose Hell, you can also choose Heaven?

There are two differences: the people on earth who choose Hell know that they will go there. But nobody is sure on the earth if they are going to Heaven or Purgatory. Not one of us is sure.

Can you be sure that you are not going to Hell?

Yes. Follow God's will. The most important thing is to know that God loves us.

How does this knowledge help us to go to Heaven?

When we know for sure that God loves us, we try to love Him in return—to respond to God's love for us by being faithful in good times and bad.[5]

Has seeing Hell changed how you pray?

Oh, yes! Now I pray for the conversion of sinners! I know what awaits them if they refuse to convert.

Has the Blessed Mother asked you to give your life for the conversion of sinners?

The Blessed Mother is asking all her children to change their lives, to pray and fast, to give their lives for the conversion of themselves and the world.

Can we judge our own holiness?

We must not try to be a judge of our own holiness. That would be just our own opinion. It's God's opinion that counts. We must pray.

What about Purgatory? Is it near Hell?

First is Heaven, then Purgatory, then Hell. It, too, is a very big space. We couldn't see people in Purgatory, just a misty, gray fog. It looked like ashes. We could sense persons weeping, moaning, trembling, in what seemed like terrible suffering. The Blessed Mother said: *"These people need your prayers, especially the ones who have no one to pray for them."* And that is why we have prayed so much for these poor souls; they desperately need our prayers, to go from Purgatory to Heaven!

Ivan has told pilgrims that the Blessed Mother said souls in Purgatory are extremely lonely. The only time they can see us on earth is during those moments we pray for them— is that true?

Yes. They can see us on earth when we pray for them, by name. Please tell people to pray for their own family members who are dead. Please tell people to pray and forgive each other, the living and the dead.

Why is forgiveness so important, Vicka?

Because not to forgive someone hurts us more than the person we won't forgive.

How does this relate to Purgatory?

I am not sure.

What must we do on earth so we don't go to Purgatory when we die?

I am not sure. . . . The Blessed Mother calls us to a holy life. The Bible shows us how.

[The following questions were asked when Vicka was suffering from her illness.]

Vicka, can you explain what the Blessed Mother has taught you about suffering?

I won't say much about suffering. It is permitted by God. When God allows sickness or some other form of suffering, it is very important to accept it with love, because it is out of His great love that God has permitted this particular suffering. If you believe in

God, you know that He knows why He allows each person's suffering. This has happened to me. I do not see my suffering as a punishment from God; I see it as a gift of love. I know it will bring joy. Its fruits are joy, not suffering. So I really do not suffer. If you take it with love, you do not suffer.

But if you take it with bitterness, you suffer a lot?

That's right.

Are you ill now?

I have suffering; painful headaches.

Why do you have this suffering?

The Blessed Mother invited me to suffer after she took me to Heaven and Hell. She then showed me Purgatory. When I heard sighing and sobbing, I asked her what those crying sounds meant. She told me that there are many religions on earth now which do not believe in Purgatory—that it really exists. Those who die in those faiths have no one to pray for them. They are quite alone and abandoned by their loved ones on earth. The Blessed Mother invited me to suffer for these abandoned souls and for the people on earth now who do not believe. I said yes, but she made me wait three days to really think about such a responsibility. After three days, she accepted my sacrifice, and I got this sickness.

Do you suffer every day?

No. Sometimes the Blessed Mother does not appear to me on certain days; when she does not come, I do not have the sickness.

Do you have sickness when you see the Blessed Mother?

Not always. When I am with her, I am in a different time frame.

How should people deal with suffering?

When God permits somebody to suffer, they should

not ask, "Why me?" He knows why. He expects love and patience from us.

What is essential is to show Him in times of troubles and difficulties that we really love Him by being faithful. We should accept the suffering as a gift, and out of love ask God if there is something more we can endure for Him.

Vicka, do you pray for the sick when you are with the Blessed Mother?

Yes. Many people come here and pray to the Blessed Mother that she ask God to cure them.

And how does the Blessed Mother respond?

The Blessed Mother always looks tenderly at the sick, very tenderly. And she tells me that the family of the sick should pray very much and believe very firmly.

Vicka, have you visionaries suffered?

Only God and the Blessed Virgin Mary know how much we have suffered—and how much more we are going to suffer. We know a little bit, but we don't care—being with the Blessed Mother every day and helping to fulfill God's plan is worth any suffering in the world!

Would you say God allows personal crosses for each of us?

Yes. How we accept that personal cross, our attitude, is about the only decision we can make. We know we can't change who our parents are, where we are born, how tall we are—things like that. God made those decisions. He knows why He chose all these things for us. We know He loves us. If we respond to His love, even what might look like a great suffering to an unbeliever is a joy. The Blessed Mother has shown me that.

What about the sick and blind, the abandoned and the dying?

When God allows sickness or blindness or other misfortunes, our attitude is what matters. God knows why He is allowing them. He knows when He is going to take them away. We have to thank God for everything, good and bad. We don't know why He does these things, because we are weak. Really, we are weak. He knows why we are suffering. My suffering is always for somebody. The Blessed Mother has taught me that we are great in His eyes, when we accept suffering with a loving heart. Our suffering is for the most needy, the people who really need it the most.

Vicka, can you tell us what the most important thing in your life is?

Yes, the Blessed Mother has led me to understand that the center of my life is the Eucharist, which is Jesus, Who is God.

Tell us about the Eucharist.

The most important thing about the Sacrament of the Eucharist is that we are receiving Jesus, Who is alive. The Sacrament is really receiving Jesus, His own Body and His own Blood. What we are receiving, though, depends on us. Are our hearts clean enough to take Him into our hearts? We must be prepared to receive Jesus alive. We must do this act consciously, knowing what it means to receive Him alive. Then we experience Jesus' real presence within us and around us.

How do we prepare to receive Him?

Before going to Holy Mass, focus intently on Who you will be receiving. During Mass open your heart to Jesus. See Him with the "eyes" of your heart. We see and experience and live with Jesus through faith. That's why, during Mass, our faith must be very strong. The stronger our faith, the better prepared we are to welcome Him in the Holy Eucharist. We must not only listen during Holy Mass, we must really experience all the holy words of the Mass with love. That's why, toward the end of Mass when you are receiving Jesus alive, if your heart is open, He is truly with you. When the Mass is ended and you go out of the church, you will be filled with unspeakable joy!

Vicka, some of these messages at Medjugorje involve chastisements for the sins of the world, don't they?

Yes. The Blessed Mother said there will be punishments for the sins of the world.

Do you know anything about the End Times, The Apocalypse?

No, nothing.

Should people be afraid?

Not if they are prepared. If we are afraid of these kinds of things, we don't have confidence in God. Fear of this kind does not come from God. It can only come from Satan who wants to disturb us, so that we close ourselves to God and are not able to pray. With God, you can only have confidence—and strength to go through any troubles.

How do we prepare?

The best preparation is to pray every day, go to Mass, and read the Bible. With prayer and penance the chastisements can be substantially lessened. I can only say: *Prepare.* For all eternity, you will thank God if you do.

Will the people who listen to the Blessed Mother and change their lives and convert have it easier during the chastisements?

Of course. That is why we are trying to lead people to conversion. We have to help people convert. We have to prepare them for the chastisement. We help them with our prayers and the things we are doing. Everything we are doing at Medjugorje is to show people the right way to live the messages.

Will God's mercy stop at some point?

If we are open to the Lord's mercy, it never stops. If you don't want God's mercy, it stops for you.

When the permanent sign comes in Medjugorje, will it be too late for many to convert?

Yes.

Will the permanent sign happen in your lifetime?

Yes.

What happens to those people who don't really believe enough right now to convert and want to wait until the permanent sign comes?

For those people, it will be too late. The Blessed Mother says that is why God is giving so much time for these apparitions, so that all may come to conversion. She wants to make certain that all people have this opportunity. She can't help anybody who doesn't want to change, who doesn't come back to God, who doesn't put God first. If you don't do this now, it will be too late.

Will they go to Hell?

They might; I don't know. I cannot answer these questions further.

Vicka, have you seen Jesus?

As far as seeing Jesus with my eyes, the first time I saw Him was at Christmas when the Blessed Mother appeared with the baby Jesus in her arms. She brings the Infant Jesus every Christmas in her arms. Two years ago on Good Friday, she showed me her Son, as He was hanging on the cross, with the crown of thorns and dressed in torn clothes, as He was when they killed Him. Then she showed me how He looked after they killed Him. She said, "I wanted you to see this, to know how much He suffered for you."

What does she want us to do for Jesus?

In the last message, the Blessed Mother said: *"I would like you to do without your favorite thing, the thing that you like the most. Especially, I would like you to refuse to sin. Please—do not sin! Do this for the love of Jesus, who loved you so much that He suffered this hideous death for you."*

The messages here at Medjugorje are getting us in touch with what the Church already teaches us.

Of course! The messages of the Blessed Mother are simply a repetition of the Gospel Jesus taught us. So many people in the world have forgotten the words of Jesus. God sent the Blessed Mother to remind us of what her Son told us. She is here to teach all her children things many have forgotten.

Has the Blessed Mother told you why God made you?

God loves everything He has made. We are very special, His creatures with free will. He loves us so much that He made us free—free to choose Him or reject Him. He has a plan for each one of us; everyone is part of His plan. And God gives each person an assignment. Those who do His will live in great peace. They experience great love, even on this earth.

[On September 25, 1988, Vicka was healed. Six months later, the author met with her again.]

Vicka, you look wonderful!

I am always filled with joy.

Can you tell us something about the physical healings which have taken place here since the apparitions began?

In the early days of the apparitions, I had a friend who used to come to the mountain every day. He had injured his leg in a farming accident; in fact, from his knee down he had no leg. The lower part of his leg was missing. But every day he would climb the mountain. We had to help him because it was difficult for him. I would see the Blessed Mother look at him and smile at him very tenderly.

Does she do that often?

From time to time I will see her smile at certain pilgrims on the hill and on the mountain in a special way.

What happened to him?

Well, once the Blessed Mother showed us a vision of his leg and promised us that she would give him a new leg.

Has his leg been healed?

Not yet. That will happen when the permanent sign comes.

How do you know?

The Blessed Mother showed us.

She showed you?

Yes. When the Blessed Mother appeared, she showed us the boy alongside her.

He was standing there?

No, he really wasn't. I don't know where he was. The Blessed Mother appeared to us with our friend beside her. He was completely in some sort of glow. He wasn't aware of this at all. The Blessed Mother told us that he would be completely healed after the great sign. This was in mid-1982.

Did the Blessed Virgin Mary tell you visionaries that, or did she tell him that?

She told us, and then we told him.

What did he say?

He told us that during the time of the apparition, he sensed a current in the injured leg, a flow of electricity through his foot.

I thought you said he didn't have a foot?

He doesn't. But he felt a flow of current or electricity in his missing foot—in the place where his foot should have been.

Then what happened?

He said he felt a great confidence and love in the Virgin Mary before, but has even more now.

Does he believe he will have a new leg?

He not only believes it, he knows it! The Blessed Virgin Mary has promised it!

Does she promise to heal everyone who asks?

Certainly not. The Blessed Mother does only God's

will. We must all do God's will. It is not the Blessed Mother who cures people. It is God who cures people.

What does the Blessed Mother say about praying for healing?

She says it is necessary to have a firm faith in God, to pray, to fast, and to do good work. But most of all, it is necessary to believe, to firmly believe and to trust. Also, she asks that the relatives of the sick pray and fast. It is really important for the family to believe firmly and to pray all the more. The Blessed Mother is always reminding us of the power of family prayer.

What exactly has she said about family prayer?

The Blessed Mother said that every member of a family must pray for each member of that family every day and must pray with each member of the family, if possible, every day. It is very important that families pray together, especially the rosary. Children should pray with parents, parents with children.

Why is praying as a family and for the family, so important?

The Blessed Mother says that praying and fasting— and especially praying the rosary as a family—are so powerful they can even stop wars.

What kind of wars?

All kind of wars—family wars, neighborhood wars, city wars, country wars.

Vicka, what about young people, especially those harmed by drugs or alcohol?

Drugs and alcohol are a big evil on this earth. We have to help these young victims with our prayers.

We can tell them that they are on the wrong path, but they must see it for themselves; their cooperation is necessary to get back on the right path.

We have to tell them? That's hard! People do not want to hear about the evils of drugs and alcohol.

I know it's hard. The Blessed Mother recommends that all people on earth pray in a special way, with special intensity for the youth in the world. They are in a serious and very difficult situation. The Blessed Mother says: *"Dear youth, what the modern world offers you is transitory. It is passing away before your eyes. When you look at the world, realize that Satan is using every single moment and opportunity for himself."* She also says, *"This is a time of great mercy."* The only way we can help the youth of the world is with our love and with prayer that comes from our hearts.

What do you know about Satan, Vicka?

One of the visionaries saw a young man. He was very good-looking to her, but he wanted her to do things contrary to what the Blessed Mother wanted her to do. She looked into his eyes, and his eyes were spinning around. She became very scared. Something was terribly wrong. She fled. Then she had an apparition. The Blessed Mother came and told her that person was Satan. Then she said that Satan does not always come as an evil-looking person, so that we can recognize him. Sometimes, he comes as a very attractive person, to deceive or distract us so that we cannot see that it is Satan. He has immense power right now.

What is his modus operandi?

He tries to make us confused. He wants us to see him as the good, to see him and his promises as a way of life. So many times he comes as a nice person who wants to give us everything with his "kindness." We accept this because we want to think it is good.

How do we know that it's him?

We can tell inside, whether something is good or evil. It's like a gut instinct. If it brings us peace, it is from God. If we are agitated or upset, we must be on guard. If we pray with the heart, we will know whether something is from God or not. If, as we pray, we experience disturbance, we need to pray harder. When we do, he sees that he is powerless and leaves us in peace.

How do we deal with him?

Every day we must ask God to keep Satan far away from us, and accept the help He gives us through His angels whom He assigns to protect us.

Is there anything else we can do?

Yes. We should wear something blessed all the time. Satan dislikes blessed objects, especially crosses and the Scapular.

Vicka, what is the role of fasting in these messages?

The Blessed Mother is asking us to fast on Wednesdays and Fridays. And she would like us first and foremost to give up something that is dear to us on those days. Persons who are healthy and say they cannot fast because they have headaches, or something like that—all I can say is, we can fast, we are strong enough, if we are doing it for love of God. Even we don't know how powerful fasting is.

What is the purpose of fasting?

Through fasting we purify our hearts.[6] In order

to have a clean heart[7], we need the grace that comes from fasting. And when we totally clean our hearts, we are able to realize the Blessed Mother's plan, and what she is expecting from us.

When fasting gets difficult, many people give up, because bread and water seems too extreme.

The first time is always the most difficult time. When we first try to fast, Satan tries hard to disturb us, to make us think, "Well, I could eat a little something extra." We have to pray hard this first time,—really hard. When we pray and when we fast, Satan can do nothing to us. The second time will be easier, and the third time even easier. Then it will become natural.

Vicka, is it important to fast on bread and water only?

That is what the Blessed Mother is requiring of me here at Medjugorje. Those who pray know how they must fast.

How does sin affect us, Vicka?

When we sin, we offend God—but we destroy ourselves.

How?

We destroy our peace and joy. We become sad—or angry. Only God can forgive us. We can confess, but each confession means we intend not to commit that sin again, but to go on living in a better way.

So when we confess, we have to make a commitment that we won't sin again?

That promise is essential. And we must totally open our hearts when we go to confession. Some say only half their sins and hide the rest. But that's not confession. We have to confess totally when we go to confession.

What about people who don't believe in confession? What are they to do?

Pray for those persons, because words cannot help them. We cannot explain to them. We can only pray, and through our prayers they can come closer to us and to believe.

Do you know why the Blessed Mother chose St James Parish?

Yes. There are no coincidences.

Do all events have significance?

Yes. Consider, for example, my name. My real name is Vida, which means "life." The Blessed Mother has told me the story of her life and asked me to write it with her help. She told me the title of the book: Life.

A book?

Yes, I have three journals.

When will it be available?

When the Blessed Mother says it. Everything is ready, everything is prepared. I am only waiting.

Does our name give us some hints about who God knows us to be?

Yes. My name Vida means Life; Ivanka and Ivan mean John. The Blessed Mother first appeared in Medjugorje on the Feast of John the Baptist. His message was "Repent, the Kingdom of Heaven is at hand." He prepared the way for the coming of the Messiah. Marija and Mirjana both mean Mary, the Blessed Mother's name, and Jacov means James. This is St James Parish.

Do you know why we have our particular names?

Yes. The Blessed Mother told me that before God made the world, He knew each of His children of the earth and named each one of us.

Don't our parents give us our names?

God names us, but He gives our parents the grace to name us with the name He has for us.

Do you think your being a visionary was a coincidence?

Nothing is a coincidence. Everything is a project of God. Before God made this world, He planned each one of us. The Blessed Mother told me He knew us. He called us by name before He made the world. Each of us is totally known and loved by God, before we are placed in our mother's womb. He selected the particular century in which we would be born, our nationality, our family, our sex, our strengths and weaknesses. Everything we are and we have from God are gifts.

How do we know that there are no coincidences?

Through faith. The Blessed Mother said faith is really a great gift that God gave to us. From day to day we have to pray for our faith to grow. The most important thing we can do now is to show people by our example, by what we do, and how we love them.

You make holiness sound so simple!

I think holiness is simply faithfulness to God in good times and bad.

The twin spires of St James.

"Sheep and lambs may safely graze. . . ."

Ivan

4

Ivan

Trust the mercy of God

Dark-featured, self-contained, and intense, Ivan
Dragicevic has served his year of compulsory military
service and returned to Medjugorje. Perhaps because
of his serious demeanor, he seems older than his
May 25, 1965, birthday would indicate. The leader
of a young people's prayer group, he also enjoys sports,
especially professional basketball.

[Ivan gave two brief personal interviews.]

* * *

*Ivan, do you still have your apparitions every day with
the Blessed Mother?*
Yes, I do.
Do you know when the permanent sign is going to come?
Yes.
Is it going to be in your lifetime?
Yes.
*When the permanent sign comes, will everybody in the
whole world believe because of the sign?*

I don't know.

Why has the Blessed Mother come?

The Blessed Mother has been permitted by God to come here. She knows what is coming in the future. She is calling all God's children back on the path to Heaven.

What is that path?

The path that Jesus told us about in the Gospels.

Ivan, were you present during the apparition on the mountain last night? (The Feast of the Assumption, August 15, 1988)

Yes, I was there with Marija.

Can you tell us about it?

The Blessed Mother appeared with three angels. She was very happy. She gave a special blessing to all the people on the mountain. She was happy that so many people had suffered much to come there to honor her on that Feast Day.

She was aware of the heat and the suffering of the pilgrims?

The Blessed Mother is aware of everything. She loves each of us, no matter what is in our hearts.

What did the Blessed Mother say during the apparition last night?

She wants everyone in the world to pray, especially for youth. She wants us to talk to youth, to guide them and bring them back to God.

What should young people do?

In my opinion, the question should be: "What should parents do?" They should have more time for their children, to give them love and guidance. They should pray together with their children, communicate with their children to solve problems together as a family. Parents should limit the freedom of children.

Children should only be as free as they are responsible. Parents are the best ones to judge how responsible their children are. Parents have the authority from God to set limits on their children's freedom.

Did the Blessed Mother talk to you about that, Ivan?

About that and much more. It is difficult with words to describe how much the Blessed Mother loves us. She is worried about the whole world. People talk so much about nuclear war, but there is nothing much that anybody is doing to stop it.

Does the Blessed Mother speak about that?

People do not need philosophy.

What do they need?

They need to live a simple life.

Does the Blessed Mother say we don't need philosophy?

The Blessed Mother says it is good to learn. But sometimes learning can cause harm.

What is the Blessed Mother telling us to do?

She is calling us to live a simple, peaceful life. We must be careful not to be seduced by the attractions of the world.

What does the Blessed Mother say about that?

She says that much of the world suffers from an illness today, and we all need to be cured.

What illness?

The illness called Materialism.

Why is it an illness?

Because it causes blindness. Materialism makes money a god. When money is a god, you can't see anything else; you are blind.

Has the Blessed Mother told you that?

Yes, this makes her very sorrowful. We need money, because we need to buy certain things. But we should use money only for basic needs.

What can we do to be healed?

Follow the Blessed Mother's messages.

Are you part of a prayer group, Ivan?

Yes.

Does the Blessed Mother prefer everyone to be part of a prayer group?

She wants prayer groups not only here, but throughout the world.

Why?

It is through prayer that we come to know God. There is much power in group prayer.

How does a prayer group begin?

It is a long procedure. It takes time to prepare the conditions for the establishment of a prayer group. The leader of the prayer group is very important. Without a good leader, the prayer group will fall apart. In my prayer group, the leader is the Blessed Mother. I am just a coordinator between the Blessed Mother and the other members. Also, the prayer group should have a definite goal. The members should have a reason to meet and pray and fast.

Does your prayer group have a goal?

Yes. The goal in my prayer group is to help the Blessed Mother to achieve God's plan. We do this through living the Blessed Mother's messages and encouraging others to live the messages.

What is God's plan for which the Blessed Mother asks your prayer group to meet and pray and fast?

The conversion of the world.

Does the Blessed Mother encourage you to go to Mass every day?

Yes. The Mass has great significance. We must become aware of what the Mass is.

Is the Mass the center of your life?

Definitely.

Do you fast on bread and water on Wednesdays and Fridays?

Yes.

Should everyone in the world do that?

Everyone should live the messages the best way for his life. Each person is different.

Ivan, can you share anything with us about the secrets?

About the secrets, I can say nothing.

Are you fearful?

No.

Do you have any plans for the future of your life?

Those decisions are private.

Do you know whether you're going to Heaven when you die, Ivan?

I have seen Heaven already.

Will you tell us about it?

Heaven is worth any cost! Jesus showed us that, with His death on the Cross. His death was not the end. He rose from the dead, glorified, to put an end to death forever for God's children. People in heaven are happy. They live in the fullness of God.

Can you explain what that means?

You'll have to experience it to know. It is better than anything you can imagine!

Have you seen Purgatory?

Yes. The Blessed Mother told me that those who go to Purgatory are those who prayed and believed only occasionally—that they were filled with doubt, that they were not certain that God exists. They did not know how to pray while on earth, or if they did know how, they did not pray.

If people believe when they die, do they have to go to Purgatory, or can they go right to Heaven?

I don't know. Souls in Purgatory suffer. If no one prays for them, they suffer even more.

Can you tell us about Hell?

I prefer not to discuss it.

What has the Blessed Mother asked you to do?

The Blessed Mother has asked me to be a witness with my life. She has asked me to obey the messages, to pray and fast, and to convey her messages to all who come to me.

How do you pray?

I pray for God's plans to be realized.

Do you know what God's plans are?

Only what the Blessed Mother has told me.

Can you share what the Blessed Mother has told you?

Yes. The Blessed Mother has told me to tell people to pray and fast, to live the messages, to return to God.

Ivan, what message would you like to give us?

Tell people to pray to God with their heart. Tell people to be confident of the love of God for all His children. Tell people to trust the mercy of God. All people in the world are being called to respond faithfully to these messages of the Mother of God. Then all people will have peace.

"Behold, I make all things new. . . ."

Gathering in the hay.

Ivan and Jacov greeting pilgrims.

5

Jacov

Experiencing God within

[Born in 1971, Jacov Colo was 17 when the author first met him.]

Sun-bleached hair, barefoot, wearing a sleeveless t-shirt and frayed shorts—Jacov Colo could remind you of a California surfer. . . . until you looked into his eyes. In them you would find a depth that belies the air of youthful nonchalance and the casual attire. Here was a young man who seemed at home in the presence of God.

When asked about Heaven, he would not respond—but for a moment something in his eyes indicated that they had gazed upon what others could only imagine.

At the same time there is something winsome and endearing about Jacov, who is slight and very shy; even if you do not know his background, you feel like giving him a hug. That background is tragic: his father abandoned his family when the boy was eight, and his mother died when he was twelve. He lives now with his aunt and uncle.

In the last interview with him, Jacov mentioned that the Blessed Mother had been explaining the future of the Church and the world to him. As he shared what she had taught him about the heart being the tabernacle of the Most High, one had a sense of her mothering him.

* * *

Jacov, would you describe your apparitions when they occur each evening?

Yes. Before the Blessed Mother arrives, her presence is preceded by a brilliant light that flashes three times. Then the Blessed Mother appears, and she always says, "Praise Jesus." After I greet her, she and I always recommend all the sick people who come here to God. Then we pray together.

How do you pray?

We pray the "Our Father" and the "Glory Be", and other prayers from our heart to God.

Could you tell us a few things about your daily apparitions?

Yes. I have a special place in my house where I pray. This is the place where the Blessed Mother appears to me. I begin the rosary every day at 6 p.m. At 6:40, the Blessed Mother arrives.

Do you always begin the rosary at home in that special place?

Yes, on most evenings. Sometimes I go to the church. Then, the Blessed Mother appears to me at the church.

What is the Blessed Mother like? Is there a word that comes to mind?

The Blessed Mother of Jesus is pure love. And the

love that she is giving me is not only for me, but for everybody in the whole world.

How do you know that?

During these years with the Blessed Mother I have personally experienced that.

Jacov, you have been visited every day of your life since you were ten by the Mother of God. How do you relate to her?

It is very hard to find the words to describe this relationship we have. I am her child, and I am a messenger of God's plan. She has explained to me that she is the mother of all people on the earth, not just me. She is available to each person on the earth. Anyone who wants, can have the Blessed Mother as his Mother, to guide him and protect him on earth and bring him home to Heaven.

Do you know much about your own future, Jacov?

The Blessed Mother has taught me many things.

Do you know whether you will go to Heaven when you die?

I have been in Heaven already.

Is it hard to live on the earth after you have been in Heaven?

I would not like to talk about my suffering.

Will you tell us about Heaven?

When you get there, then you will see how it is.

You have said that the reason the Blessed Mother took you there was to show you what it would be like for those who remain faithful to God—would you tell us any more?

If I thought about it too much—I would die of loneliness.

Jacov, have you been in Purgatory?

The Blessed Mother showed Vicka and me Purgatory, but I have not been in it.

You have said that Purgatory is a place where souls are purified—do you pray for them?

Yes.

Do you suggest that others pray for them?

Yes. As an act of love.

Do you think it is pleasing to God?

All prayer is pleasing to God.

Jacov, did you see Hell?

Yes.

Can you tell us about it?

Very seldom do I talk about Hell.

Why?

I choose not to think about Hell. The self-chosen suffering there is beyond your ability to comprehend.

Does it cause you pain?

More than you can understand.

Why?

Because no one needs to go to Hell. It is the ultimate waste.

What can people do to keep from going to Hell?

Believe in God, no matter what happens in a lifetime.

What about your life, Jacov?

I have to be a witness with my life to others.

Does the Blessed Mother seem worried about the West— the United States in particular?

The Blessed Mother has come here and is suffering because of the godlessness in the whole world, not just because of Yugoslavia or some other specific country.

Do you know whether we are coming into the times referred to as the End Times?

My role is not as a prophet. I am a witness to the messages the Blessed Mother is bringing to the whole world here at Medjugorje.

Does the Blessed Mother talk to you about personal things?
Yes. If she has something special to tell me, she talks about it to me.
Do you ask her questions?
I talk to her.
How does the Blessed Mother treat you? Is the relationship like one between a mother and a son, or does she treat you more like an instrument through whom her messages from God are communicated to the world?
Both of these components are the same.
In what way?
When the Blessed Mother gives messages to me for the world, I must spread these messages to others. Then I am an instrument of God. But, of course, I am always the beloved child of the Blessed Virgin Mary. All of us on the earth are her beloved children. That I know from personal experience.
Have you ever touched the Blessed Mother?
Yes.
Could you describe that?
There are no words to describe what it feels like to touch or be touched by the Mother of God. The experience is not of this earth.
Is her "body" a light apparition, or is it real?
The Blessed Mother has a real body. It is three-dimensional, but there is nothing about the Blessed Virgin Mary that is like anything I've ever seen before—her radiance, her greeting, her smile, her immense beauty.
Has the Blessed Mother ever kissed you?
Yes. That experience is part of the things of Heaven.
Do you know if the Blessed Virgin Mary loves everyone or just good people?
It is beyond our comprehension now to under-

stand how very much she loves each person on the earth.

Why?

Because she is the Mother of each person on the earth.

Why is she the Mother of each person on earth?

Because the last gift Jesus gave us from the Cross before he died was His mother. Jesus' death opened the door to Heaven for all mankind, whether they know of Jesus or not. And Jesus gave His mother to be the mother of all mankind, whether they know it or not.

There are many people who are neglecting their Heavenly Mother because they don't know they have a Heavenly Mother.

But the Blessed Mother is not neglecting any one of her children. She is faithful to God. She loves and nurtures and prays for each of her children on earth, whether they know of her or not.

What does the Blessed Mother want, Jacov?

The Blessed Mother is calling us all to change our lives. She is asking the whole world to come back to God.

How are people in the world to come back to God?

Through these messages of peace, which are: faith, prayer, penance, fasting, conversion, and reconciliation.

Have you made any decisions about your future life, Jacov?

Not yet. That decision is private.

Do you go to Mass daily?

Yes. The Blessed Mother has taught me to make the Mass the center of my life.

Do you fast on bread and water on Wednesdays and Fridays?

Yes.

Do you have all ten secrets, Jacov?

No, only nine.

Do you know when the permanent sign is going to come?

Yes.

Is it going to be in your lifetime?

That is a secret.

Based on what you know now, do you personally think everyone in the world should believe and convert right now?

That is why the Blessed Mother is here. She is asking all people in the world to change their lives and turn back to God.

Do you have any message for the youth of the world?

Yes. They should realize the situation in which they are today. It is urgent that young people respond to the Blessed Mother's messages. Those who do will never be able to thank God enough.

What role do parents have in the Blessed Mother's messages?

Their role is very important. In early childhood, the parents' example forms the child. You can't start raising children when they are twenty years old. A young person needs an example to follow.

Do you have any advice for families, Jacov?

If the family has money, if the family has many things, do not allow the family to get used to everything. Limit the use of luxuries. Practice self-discipline, live in moderation. And pray together, especially the rosary. You must put God first in your life.

Jacov, what is penance?

It is kind of like a sacrifice. Look at penance the same way you look at fasting.

Can you give us an example?

Yes. A penance is to go to the Mountain of the Cross and climb it in prayer instead of resting or relaxing. Or to go to visit a relative instead of a friend. To do things to please God, instead of pleasing ourselves.

How does a young person fast, Jacov?

The same way as adults fast. I have fasted on bread and water only on Wednesdays and Fridays since I was ten, because the Blessed Mother asked me to fast that way. You have to fast with the intention to love God. It is the love that makes the fasting valuable.

Has the Blessed Mother ever mentioned television?

Yes. Television can be looked at as a way of fasting, of giving up something for the love of God. That is, enjoyment can be sacrificed for the love of God.

The Blessed Mother wants us to give up enjoyment?

She wants us to do without something that is important to us, for the love of God.

Jacov, can you describe a typical day in your life?

I don't do anything special. I get up, go to work, go home, just like any other person. We have our daily routines.

Does the Blessed Mother want you to go to daily Mass?

Yes. She would like that for everybody in the world. Not just me, but everybody in the world.

Why?

Because the Mass should be the center of our lives. That is the most important gift we have in God's house, the church, and that is where we should be.

If you don't go to Mass, does the Blessed Mother reprimand you?

The Blessed Mother never says anything to reprimand me. I have free will which the Blessed Mother deeply respects. She leaves my choices up to me.

Have you ever done anything wrong which she has spoken to you about?

Yes. She will mention things to me.

Has she ever been firm with you?

That is private!

Does she promise to stay here in Medjugorje the rest of your life?

My apparitions have not yet ceased. That part is decided toward the end. I still have the daily apparitions. Nothing is yet decided.

Has the Blessed Mother ever missed a day appearing to you?

Ever since June 24, 1981, she has missed only five days.

Did you know in advance that the Blessed Mother would not come?

No.

Were you disappointed when she didn't come?

I was very sad.

Do you think she was punishing you?

No. It has nothing to do with that. It was in the beginning. I don't remember details. It was not because I did something wrong.

Does the Blessed Mother have personal messages for you, or just messages for the world?

Mostly we pray together. We recommend all the poor, the sick, and the needy to God. It is daily prayer that we share.

What does conversion mean to you, Jacov?

When I was small, I only knew about God. I went to church, but I never really experienced God. I went through the motions. God has to live within you. I didn't experience that until this apparition happened.

How does God live within you now?

I would explain conversion to mean: God living within me, and me being aware of it.

What does it mean to have God living within?

You can experience it through prayer. You can feel God's presence within you through prayer.

Is the whole world called to this awareness?

Yes. That is what the Blessed Mother is here to teach us—that awareness of God's presence within each of us on the earth.

Is this awareness possible for every person on earth?

Yes. The Blessed Mother says that with prayer, everybody on earth can experience God's presence within.

What about people who have never heard of Jesus?

The Blessed Mother has said it is up to us to tell them about Him, and it is up to them to accept Him. You can never force anyone to believe. It is up to all of us to be messengers of this truth.

Would you say giving time to God is a way for people to begin to experience God within?

That is the way to conversion—to put time aside for prayer.

Does the Blessed Mother tell you about the future of the world?

Yes.

Can you tell us anything about it?

No.

How long are your apparitions?

Between two and five minutes.
Is the future of the world happy or sad?
I can't speak about that.
What does our Blessed Mother want, Jacov?
She wants everyone on earth to want Heaven. The Blessed Mother says the way to Heaven is through prayer.

Confession

Marija

6

Marija

Each individual chooses his eternity

Born in 1965, Maria Pavlovic is a natural leader. When she speaks (even casually around the supper table), others listen. She has a gentle, quiet, loving spirit, and her inner joy is evident in the sparkle in her eye. Since 1984, she has been receiving messages for the entire world on the 25th of each month.

[The author had four interviews with Marija. By coincidence, the first was on the eve of her departure for a four-month prayer retreat in Italy, and the second was immediately upon her return. The last two occurred in Birmingham, Alabama, where she underwent successful kidney transplant surgery on behalf of her brother.]

To spend time with Marija is to come into a new appreciation of the perfection of God's love. Perfect love casts out all fear[1], and to see God's plan through Marija's eyes is to know that those who love God need fear nothing.

Marija, would you tell us about the Blessed Mother?

I see the Blessed Mother every day. She is inviting us to respond to her message of faith, conversion, penance, fasting twice a week, prayer, sacramental life, confession once a month, and putting the Mass at the center of our lives. And the Blessed Mother is inviting us each day to enter more deeply in our response to Her request.

Can you tell us how we are to enter more deeply?

The Blessed Mother is encouraging us to pray more and more every day.

What kind of prayer?

The Blessed Mother has said that every prayer said with the heart is acceptable and pleasing to God.

How do you pray with your heart?

The Blessed Mother has said that we are to give time, sincerely give time, to God. If we put aside a special time each day for God, then the sincerity with which we give Him space in our lives will begin to bear fruit, and we will know how to pray with sincere hearts.

What does the Blessed Mother look like?

The Blessed Mother comes every evening dressed in a gray dress and a white veil. She has black wavy hair and blue eyes, her feet are in a cloud, and there is a crown of twelve stars around her head.

Does she look the same each time, Marija?

Usually she is dressed the same, except on feast days, when she wears a golden tunic. Once on Mount Krizevac gold was radiating through and from her clothes.

Has she ever touched you or held you or kissed you?

Yes, I touched her many times, and I have been kissed by her. I do have physical contact with the Blessed Mother.

When you hug her, do you feel as if you are hugging a real flesh-and-blood person?

Yes. We have a close relationship, a great friendship with the Blessed Mother. Each of her visits is a great joy! We are happy, even when the Blessed Mother is sad. Many times the Blessed Mother cried, and each time she asks us to take her messages seriously, convert and change our lives. Even when she cries, we are still filled with joy—because we realize what a great grace it is that the Blessed Mother wants to be with us, to speak with us. It is a tremendous joy! Even her crying does not take away from this joy.

Does she have a feeling of love for the other children in the world, or is it just special to you visionaries?

The Blessed Mother always says she loves each one of her children on the earth with the same love. She has no preferential love. She loves each person in the world in the same way that she is loving us, but through us it is a manifestation of her individual love for each one of her children.

Has the Blessed Mother told you how the rest of the world can feel her love?

Yes. The Blessed Mother promises that with prayer we all can, little by little, feel God's love for us and her love for us. The way to experience this great love is through prayer.

What about the people who don't know how to pray?

The Blessed Mother has said that we can help them by our prayers, because our prayers will bring us to know God, and they will be able to recognize God through us. Jesus has said that if two or three pray together, He is there with them.

Marija, why do so many people not know God?

The Blessed Mother has often said that each one

of us is free, and with our freedom we can choose to come to know God, or we can choose to be opposed to Him.

Does everyone in the world have a chance to know God?

Yes. The Blessed Mother says that everyone has that opportunity. We must pray for those who do not know God and give example with our own lives, so that the more we come to know Him, the easier it is for the others to know Him through us.

Do you know, Marija, why the Blessed Mother comes here to you, rather than to some other person elsewhere?

We asked the Blessed Mother that in the beginning, and she said that the Eternal Father allowed her to select where she wanted to choose the children of the world for this manifestation of His plan. She decided to choose here.

Did she say why?

Yes. She said it was the Eternal Father's will. She told us that whenever we are given a grace like this, we have to respond. It's not the choosing that is important; it is the response that is important. We are free to choose to respond or not. This is a gift. We are happy to respond.

Does the Blessed Mother make this invitation to every living person in the world?

Yes. Everyone is being called to respond to this message. The response depends on our own freedom. God does not press us to respond, so we have a choice.

Is the message for Hindus and Buddhists, for Jews and Protestants, Moslems and atheists? Is it meant for everyone on earth?

Yes. The message is for everyone who wants to live!

How do we respond to this message of Medjugorje?

The Blessed Mother says we must pray, and through prayer we will come to know God and her, and we will know what path God wants us to take. The Blessed Mother has said the Holy Mass should be the center of our lives. For many, it is not the center, because they do not know yet what God's will is. She says that we can always grow closer to God. By growing closer to God, there could come a time when we do truly understand that the Holy Mass is the center of our lives.

What does the Mass mean to you, Marija?

For me, there is this understanding that Holy Mass should be the center of our lives. This is our way of coming closer to God through the Blessed Mother, because we're responding to her message. She has asked us to make Mass the center.

Was the Mass always the center of your life?

Oh no! When the Blessed Mother first began to teach me to pray, she asked me to pray seven Our Fathers and Glory Be's every day.

How did you respond?

I said, "Oh, Holy Mother, I could never pray that many prayers on one day! I don't have time!"

How much do you pray now?

I have offered my entire life as a prayer to God.

Marija, has the Blessed Mother taught you about Jesus?

Yes, in everything the Blessed Mother is speaking of Jesus. We have begun to understand that the Blessed Mother is here to help us little by little to come closer to Jesus. She is here for Jesus, to bring us to Jesus.

Do you feel that you have become closer to Jesus, through Mary?

I know I have become closer to Jesus through the Blessed Mother! It is easier and faster to come close to Jesus through Mary than any other way.

Would you tell us about Jesus?

The Blessed Mother has always said that Jesus is the center of our life. In the first days of the apparitions, the center of our life was the Blessed Mother. But afterwards, she guided us, and she said that Jesus must be the center of our lives. For us— it was to discover Jesus and come closer to Jesus.

Do you know why Jesus was crucified?

It was His way of demonstrating His love for us. He gave His life for us.

Do you think that part of our problem is that we do not know how much Jesus loves us?

The Blessed Mother says we have to pray in order to come to know the great mystery of God's love for us.

What is the reason so many people in the world don't love God?

Many times people don't know Jesus, because Christians aren't giving a good example of Him. They are not bringing Jesus to others. This is why the Blessed Mother is coming first to us as Christians, because she's trying to teach us how to get back on the right path, so that through our changed lives we can help our brothers and sisters to know Jesus and the Eternal Father better.

Do you think about the Blessed Mother and Jesus all the time?

Yes. Every day I try to grow deeper in my relationship with Jesus and Mary.

Is it hard for you to work, if you want to pray all the time?

The Blessed Mother has said that our work can become prayer.

How does that happen?

She says that if we offer our work with joy to the Eternal Father, then the work becomes a prayer. Prayer is communication. If we are joyfully giving our work, and God is receiving it—this is a form of communication. And since communication is prayer, then any work joyfully given is prayer.

So, even if our work is unpleasant or not to our liking, it is something that can be pleasing to the Heavenly Father?

Yes. We can always offer our work. If it is something that gives us suffering or something that is difficult, we can offer our work as a sacrifice to God. So, instead of concentrating on whether it pleases us or not, we want to work as a gift. We want to do it better, because it is a gift that we are offering to God. And so, this sacrifice becomes our prayer and can help us to grow in holiness.

Marija, regarding people caught in difficult marital relationships, would you suggest that in a sacramental marriage it is important to stay in the marriage and offer it as a sacrifice to God, trusting that He will make all things well?

Yes. But we have to do this with a great deal of prayer. If we look to Jesus' life, it was a great sacrifice for Him to take up His cross and go the way to Calvary, to die for us. But it was not the sacrifice that pushed Him to Calvary; it was love that pushed Him to Calvary! In responding to this marital issue, we must pray much so that love is what guides our decision. Love is what brings man peace.

Marija, do you know why God made you?

I've understood it like this: God's love is very great.

And in His love He even created me. I am fruit of His love. God has given us a special gift; He wants to love us more than Himself. He has given us freedom by which we can choose to respond to His love. Our life isn't just a moment. It's a path that we have, so that we can go to Heaven.

What do you mean God loves us more than Himself?

He loves us because we are His creatures. He made us in His own image and likeness.

If He is seeking our love back, and has given us free will, then we have the capacity to hurt Him?

We do have the capacity of hurting God, in the sense that God is doing everything. He even sent His Son and allowed Him to die for us, to show us how much He loves us. He created us to respond to His love. And so it is true in the sense that, with our freedom, we can choose not to love God, not to respond to His great love for us.

Marija, did you see the Blessed Mother last night during her apparition on the mountain? (The Feast of the Assumption, August 15, 1988)

Yes I did. She was dressed in a beautiful dress of gold. She appeared with three angels. She was very pleased.

Did she bless all the people on the hill?

Yes. She blessed all the people who were present on the hill.

Did she say anything about the people who were present?

She was very happy about their presence. She blessed them and prayed over them, because she wanted to give them all a special blessing to take back to all the different places in the world where they live.

Marija, do you know under whose authority the Blessed Mother gives such blessings?

Yes. The Blessed Mother is here, because she has a mission. She was sent here to Medjugorje by the Eternal Father. It is God's will that she is the Mother of Jesus Christ. She is the Mother of the Body of Christ. She is the Queen of Heaven. She is the Queen of the Cosmos.

What does that mean?

God has made her the Queen of all Created Things.

Marija, did the Blessed Mother have any special messages about youth?

Yes. The Blessed Mother has dedicated these next years to the conversion of the youth of the world. She has asked all people to pray at the conclusion of the Mass, or at their own worship service, for all young people in the world. The Blessed Mother gave us all a special blessing. She has asked every one of us who has that special blessing to pass it on to anyone we encounter in our lives, especially the youth. The Blessed Mother asks us to pray with great intensity and with a great spirit of self-sacrifice, for the youth of the world. She told us that in these times the youth of the world has great need for our prayers.

Marija, are there any suggestions you can give those who might be working with youth?

Yes. Pray and fast for them. We should show them the right way by our example.

What about rock music?

The Blessed Mother didn't say anything about rock music.

Marija, do you have an opinion about music?

Yes. My opinion is that rock music is more negative than positive. Diabolic messages could be transferred through this rock music.

Marija, can you tell us what the devil is like, and what things we should look for?

The devil comes in different forms. It's up to us to see it.

How do we see it? What do you have to do to be able to detect the devil?

Pray.

Pray?

Just pray.

What's the most beautiful thing, Marija, that the Blessed Mother has ever said to you?

It is very difficult to say, because every meeting with the Blessed Mother is beautiful. And the next one is more beautiful than the previous one.

Do you recommend that we pray to the Saints?

If we pray to the Saints, we become closer to God. Any prayer brings us closer to God.

What is your opinion about people with severe illnesses?

We must always pray to know God's will. It's normal that we want our friends and relatives to be healed, but if it is not God's will, no amount of praying we can do can change that.

Why are some people who come to Medjugorje healed, and others aren't? Why are some who pray at home healed and others aren't?

Illnesses and sicknesses are sort of secret mysteries. We don't know why we have illness. But if there is no illness, there is no death. If there is no death, there is no salvation. If there is no salvation, there is no Heaven. I am happy to know that there is a Heaven, and I know where I am going if I die tomorrow. The most important thing is that we know that God exists, and we believe in God. And we know there is no definite death for us. That's why we have to thank Him all the time.

Do you know if it is important to wear the Brown Scapular?

The Blessed Mother says we should wear blessed things on our body as protection against the devil.

Does the Blessed Mother say anything about the unity of all the churches?

Yes. She asks us to pray for the unity of the churches.

Is the use of the rosary a universal request, since it is so traditionally Roman Catholic?

Yes. It is a request from the Blessed Mother. She recommends that all people on earth pray the rosary, no matter what their religion or what their belief.

Do you know if this is the Blessed Mother's last apparition on earth?

Yes. The Blessed Mother said that this is her last apparition on earth, where we can touch her, see her, and talk to her.

Do you know why?

After the secrets are realized, the Blessed Mother will not need to come anymore.

Should that frighten us?

No. No one should be frightened. The Blessed Mother is here as the Queen of Peace to show us the way to peace, to bring us to God.

Well, Marija, that is easier for you than for us; you see her every day.

The Blessed Mother has said, *Blessed are they who do not see but who believe.*

How can we put that statement into practice?

Very simple: Pray to see the Blessed Mother with the eyes of faith; then you will see her.

How do you know that?

The Blessed Mother has taught me that truth.

Does that mean if we pray and have faith, we will see the Blessed Mother with our earthly eyes?

I could never answer that question. I would not know that.

Then, Marija, how will we see the Blessed Mother?

If you pray and have faith, you, too, will see and hear the Blessed Mother with the eyes and ears of faith.

How hard do we have to pray to see the Blessed Mother with the eyes and ears of faith?

Begin simply. Nothing extraordinary. Begin to pray.

Can you suggest some prayers?

The Blessed Mother has said that at a minimum we should pray at least seven "Our Father's" and seven "Glory Be's", plus the Creed. When the apparitions first began, she told us that. I thought I would never have time to say so many prayers in one day. Now I want to pray all the time. You see how it is with prayer. The important thing is to begin—then you, too, will want to pray more and more. The more you pray, the deeper your faith is. The deeper your faith is, the closer you are to God and the Blessed Mother. Then you, too, will see and hear with the eyes and ears of faith.

Marija, after all these years of seeing the Blessed Mother every day, what would you feel most compelled to share with us?

The Blessed Mother wants to lead each of us to God. She wants us to find the utmost security in God. She wants us to really trust God in every circumstance of our lives.

Is the Blessed Mother here for everyone on earth, even those who don't know Jesus?

The Blessed Mother told me that she is the mother of all people, and that she loves everyone in the world with the same love.

Why has the Blessed Mother been with us for such a long time at Medjugorje?

The Blessed Mother is here calling all the faithful of the world to conversion. She wants every one of her children in Heaven.

How should the faithful respond?

The Blessed Mother asks us to totally surrender to the will of God in our lives. In my life, I have done this. I have allowed the Blessed Mother to very deliberately direct my life. And because of that, I have grown in my love for God and, in the process, in my union with God.

If we surrender ourselves to God, is there a clear direction from God in our lives about how to live?

There is a very clear direction from God: we should surrender to God as much as possible from day to day and moment to moment, falling totally within His will for us at all times.

Did people ever mock you when you first began to pray and respond to the Blessed Mother's message?

All of us have had some suffering.

Marija, do you know anything about the chastisements that are supposedly a part of these messages of Medjugorje?

I would not like to talk about chastisements.

Do you know whether AIDS is a chastisement from God?

The Blessed Mother has never mentioned anything about AIDS to me. She has never said anything about AIDS being a chastisement from God. But the message God can give to us concerning AIDS is: purity before marriage, purity after marriage, purity in our relationships, and freedom from drug addiction.

Marija, how do you suggest we lead a lifestyle that will be both pleasing to God and give us happiness on the earth?

Just obey the ten commandments that God has given to us and lead the Christian way of life.

Can you comment on drugs?

I have spent most of my time recently with young people who were in serious difficulty. That is, they used to be on drugs, and they had AIDS. This group came and stayed with us in Italy. Part of this group, in a response to these messages of the Blessed Mother, devoted its life to prayer, to fasting, to healthy life, to working in the fields. They worked hard with their hands in the fields, they ate natural food—healthy food, and they slept well at night. They were under the supervision of a nun who was very firm in demanding a rigorous life of discipline in all bodily habits and all prayer habits. After several months of this lifestyle, when these people were examined, there were no traces of the illness of AIDS. For those, however, who did not pray and fast as the Blessed Mother asked, and work rigorously with the body, they still had AIDS. I was with those young people who had AIDS, and the doctors can't give an opinion, but the young people devoted themselves to prayer, and the deeper they became involved in their prayer life, the less they had the physical side effects of AIDS.

What does your experience with the victims of AIDS mean?

Those who didn't stay with prayer died. Our body is struggling for life. If you're going to do things to your body like taking drugs and destroying your health, then you will die, because your body, your organs can't function. That is illness. AIDS is really a message that God wants to give to us about how He wants us to live.

Marija, what is your source for this?

My source for this is the prayer life I lived in Italy with the people who had AIDS. Those who responded to the messages of the Blessed Mother at Medjugorje lived. They are well again. Those who did not respond died.

Can you tell us anything else about your time in Italy?

Sometimes when I would watch TV, I would see the different commercials, especially about how to protect from AIDS. My opinion is that the TV commercials were more interested in selling things than in protecting against AIDS. They were taking advantage of this illness. God is really our Master, and we should surrender ourselves to God. We should give ourselves to God with everything we have, and He will reward us. Many times these commercials try to frighten us, to induce us more and more to want the material things that cost money. God is our Master, and we should surrender to Him. He is the Master of every situation.

Marija, do you have an opinion about people who are ill with AIDS?

Yes. We should never judge people who have AIDS.

We should never judge anyone. We should never reject anyone, especially the sick. We should never isolate them or refuse to take care of them. That is not what God wants.

Does that mean there are no precautions medical personnel should take when dealing with this disease?

We must never go to extremes. For example, if I were to climb to the tenth floor and throw myself from the balcony and say that nothing can happen to me, that God will protect and take care of me, we know that is a sin. God expects us to use our good sense at all times in everything that we do. However, think about a place like Lourdes: the sick come from all over the world and are immersed in the waters there, and no one ever gets sick, because Lourdes is a healing place of God. We really shouldn't have any fear; we are children of God.

Do you feel it is correct for medical personnel to take precautions when dealing with contagious diseases?

I am not a scientist. All I can say is, I believe in God, I believe in God's love for me, and I believe God takes care of me. But I also know God wants me to obey Him, and He speaks through many people, even doctors.

What do you suggest that people do?

We should all respond the way we feel it is right for us to respond in our hearts and souls. We should pray, and the more deeply we pray, the more we will know what God wants us to do. We are Christians. What kind of Christians are we, if we see a man dying from AIDS, and we just run away and say, "No, he is ill. He is dying from AIDS. I want to run away. I want to protect myself. I don't care about him, let him die." An attitude like that is not a Christian attitude; it is not Christ-centered. Christ died for him, too. And we know that our lives on earth are not all that we have. We know that death is not the end of our life. It is just the beginning. Death is the beginning of our life in Heaven. We should always respond to everything on the earth as Christ taught us.

There are so many problems in the world right now, it is often very difficult to make decisions about how to respond to all the problems.

It is important that we respond to the place where we happen to be, at the place where we happen to be, in a Christian way.

Marija, what is your opinion about suffering? Should a person pray to be healed, or should a person accept himself the way he is?

One should always pray that he be able to recognize what God's will is. Then he will know how to pray.

Would you tell us about Purgatory?

Yes. Purgatory is a large place. It is foggy. It is ash gray. It is misty. You cannot see people there. It is as if they are immersed in deep clouds. You can feel that the people in the mist are traveling, hitting each other. They can pray for us but not for themselves. They are desperately in need of our prayers. The Blessed Mother asks us to pray for the poor souls in Purgatory, because during their life here, one moment they thought there was no God, then they recognized Him, then they went to Purgatory where they saw there is a God, and now they need our prayers. With our prayer we can send them to Heaven.

The biggest suffering that souls in Purgatory have is that they see there is a God, but they did not accept Him here on earth. Now they long so much to come close to God. Now they suffer so intensely, because they recognize how much they have hurt God, how many chances they had on earth, and how many times they disregarded God.

Did the Blessed Mother tell you anything about babies who are not baptized before they die?

The Blessed Mother once appeared with many children. I think those might be the children, the babies whom the Blessed Mother carried to Heaven.

Marija, have you ever seen Hell?

Yes, it's a large space with a big sea of fire in the middle. There are many people there. I particularly noticed a beautiful young girl. But when she came near the fire, she was no longer beautiful. She came out of the fire like an animal; she was no longer human. The Blessed Mother told me that God gives us all choices. Everyone responds to these choices. Everyone can choose if he wants to go to Hell or not. Anyone who goes to Hell chooses Hell.

Marija, how and why does a soul choose Hell for himself for all eternity?

In the moment of death, God gives us the light to see ourselves as we really are. God gives freedom of choice to everybody during his life on earth. The one who lives in sin on earth can see what he has done and recognize himself as he really is. When he sees himself and his life, the only possible place for him is Hell. He chooses Hell, because that is what he is. That is where he fits. It is his own wish. God does not make the choice. God condemns no one.

We condemn ourselves. Every individual has free choice. God gave us freedom.

Marija, what about people who grow up spiritually deceived, people who have been told that God does not exist, that there is no God?

People, as they grow up, can think. Everyone knows and can recognize what is good and what is bad by the time they grow up. God gives us freedom of choice. We can choose good or bad. Everybody chooses here in this life whether he goes to Heaven or Hell.

How do we choose Heaven or Hell or Purgatory for ourselves, Marija?

At the moment of death, God gives everyone the grace to see his whole life, to see what he has done, to recognize the results of his choices on earth. And each person, when he sees himself in the divine light of reality, chooses for himself where he belongs. Every individual chooses for himself what he personally deserves for all eternity.

How do we live so that we feel confident to choose Heaven when we die?

The most important thing is that we know that God exists, that we believe in God, that we trust God's love for us, and that we know there is no definite death for us. That is why we have to thank Him all the time.[2]

The Queen of the Cosmos
is God's most loving gift to all His children.
She brings Eternal Life to all His lost children.
She is His most faithful, most trusted servant.
Her love for all His children is God's love.
God's will is that
all people throughout His world
know the plan He has
to restore His kingdom on earth.
His most beloved creature,
Mary,
the Mother He has given to all His children
through His Son Jesus,
brings His plan to our globe now.
Mary is virtue.
All God's children
are called to be like her.
All are called to accept the great plan
she brings from God,
to restore His kingdom on earth.

Father Philip presides at English Mass.

7

Father Philip

"If he has will. . . "

Of Croatian background, Philip Pavich, O.F.M., is the only American-born priest associated with St James parish. He celebrates the English-language Mass and acts as liaison to English-speaking pilgrims. In this interview he describes how he left the Holy Land in 1987, to serve in Medjugorje.

* * *

Fr. Philip, do you believe the Mother of Jesus is appearing here?

Yes, I certainly do.

How did you come to believe this?

When I first heard of the Blessed Mother's apparition in Medjugorje, the thing that caught my attention was the date of the first apparition: June 24, 1981. The Feast of John the Baptist—that was my ordination day!

Why was that so significant?

First, I was ordained on that day in 1957, so St John the Baptist was my patron of priesthood, and

I had come to love him very much. Many times during my eleven years in the Holy Land, I would take pilgrim groups to Ein Kerem (a suburb of modern Jerusalem) where he was born and spend hours explaining about him. I came to see him as a revealer of Jesus Christ, because he said these very significant words, recorded in all four Gospels: "There is God's lamb who will baptize in the Holy Spirit and fire." Since every priest ought to be a revealer of Jesus, I was happy to have him as a patron.

Then there was the manner in which the Blessed Mother appeared. It was like a St John the Baptist gesture: she was holding a baby in her arms, revealing Him, as it were, to the Visionaries, and at the same time inviting them to come to Him. I thought right away that the Blessed Mother had deliberately chosen that day to come with a message of peace, faith, conversion, prayer and fasting in the spirit of St John the Baptist; it could not have been just a coincidence. Then I thought: "Those kids couldn't invent something so profound," and I was convinced; it had to be true.

So it was the Biblical appreciation of the role of John, and the manner of the Blessed Mother's actions that convinced you?

Very much so. And there was more besides.

What else?

I also guided many groups to Mount Tabor, where Jesus was transfigured. There, where Moses and Elijah had appeared conversing with Jesus, I saw that the great Lawgiver, Prophet and Priest were also "revealers" of Jesus. They were His Old Testament witnesses, just as Peter, James, and John were New Testament witnesses. But Elijah, whose name in

Hebrew means "My God is the Lord," was the link to John the Baptist. He also served as a great "revealer" of the living God in his famous challenge to the false priests of Baal on Mt. Carmel.[1] The Israelites were confused and no longer knew who the true God was—much like people today. So Elijah, by his sacrifice "acceptable to God," revealed the true God and won a people now eager to serve Him, exclaiming, "The Lord is God! The Lord is God!"

How is he linked with John the Baptist?

As they came down the mountain, Peter, James and John were puzzled at having seen Elijah, for at the end of the Old Testament Malachai prophesies that Elijah will be sent "before the coming of the great and dreadful day of the Lord."[2] Knowing that the Jews always expected Elijah to precede the Messiah's coming, they asked, in effect: "How come you're already here, Jesus, and Elijah hasn't come, as he's supposed to?" Then Jesus links him with John the Baptist and says, "Elijah is indeed coming, and he will restore everything. I assure you, though, that Elijah has already come, but they did not recognize him, and they did as they pleased with him. The Son of Man will suffer at their hands in the same way. The disciples then realized that he had been speaking to them about John the Baptizer."[3]

And the link with the Blessed Mother?

Just as Jesus showed His disciples how John the Baptist was a "restorer" and "revealer" of Himself, the Blessed Mother comes to restore the Church, to win a people eager to serve her Son—to totally surrender, as she so often says.

How did you come to Medjugorje?

Very briefly, I started praying fervently on my

rooftop overlooking the Sea of Galilee. I started asking Jesus, "Lord, what am I doing here? You were the shepherd and pastor here. This was Your parish where people were following You around the lake from one side to the other. But it seems as if hardly anyone is looking for You here anymore. Where are they?" And it was as if an answer came to me: "They are going to Medjugorje."

And that's when you started wanting to go to Medjugorje, too?

That's right! I went to a 6,000-member priests' retreat in Rome during October, 1984. An Irish Franciscan, Fr. Desmond O'Malley from Galway, was going from there to Medjugorje with about 150 priests. I felt so drawn to go to Medjugorje—but I thought the Blessed Mother had called me to the Holy Land. So I asked Fr. Desmond to inquire, if possible, through a Visionary, if the Blessed Mother wanted me to come and serve in Medjugorje, since I am American-born, already a Franciscan, of Croatian immigrant parents.

Was he able to ask one of the Visionaries for you?

Yes, amazingly he did. Through Ivan, I got an answer which Fr. Desmond sent to me some months later. It was in broken English, but it spoke to my heart: "If he has will, to come to help us to spread God's message!"

So that's how you transferred to Medjugorje?

Yes, I prayed a great deal, and eventually the Blessed Mother opened all the doors; I was given permission to serve in Medjugorje. I even joined the Franciscan Province here, so I could stay forever, God willing.

Do you sometimes miss the Holy Land, Father?

Not really, because it's like I'm still in the Holy Land. I feel as though I've just been called from "the"

Holy Land to another Holy Land. For me, Medjugorje has a wonderful, mystical meaning and it's own "Holy Land geography." The name Medjugorje means "between the mountains"—we're surrounded by mountains on every side. The Blessed Mother by her apparition has given it a new, mystical meaning, as it were: "the Church between the mountains." St James Church is symbolic of the Body of Christ. Through the work of the Holy Spirit, and with Mary as our Mother, it draws its life from, and proceeds from, "the mountains" of the Apparition and the Cross. To me, these mountains symbolize the "work of the Father" and the "work of the Son"—a true Holy Land.

And they are the main goals of pilgrims.

Very much so. Pilgrims always go to Apparition Hill, which is like an invitation to accept the great gift of the Father, who so loved the world that He gave His Son,[4] as it were, to the woman. And in the fullness of time, she so loved us that she gave "their" Son to the world.[5] Here I see the joyful mysteries and the "work of the Father." Then they always climb Cross Mountain, which is the central symbol of Medjugorje. Built by the parishioners in 1933, it shows the work of Jesus, redeeming the human race and defeating Satan and drawing us all to Himself,[6] and to His Mother to become our Mother, so that being born of her we could be His Bride Body.[7] Thus, the sorrowful mysteries and the "work of the Son." Then the Church of St James, symbolizing the "work of the Spirit," where we continue to be mothered by Mary into the Body of Christ, her Son, and thus into "the rest of her offspring." So the glorious mysteries and the "work of the Spirit." Mary is full partner of God the Father, Son, and Spirit, and present in all three places. So, for me Medjugorje is truly a holy and mystical land, where mercies and graces are flowing abundantly, bonding us to our Triune and All Holy God, and to Mary, the Mother of God.

You certainly seem to be responding to her invitation.

Yes. By hearing many hours of confessions, counseling and preaching, I have daily opportunities to live her invitation to "spread God's message." I am so grateful she first called me to the Holy Land to prepare, so I could give teachings rooted in the Bible, which is God's loving message to all mankind. And now to do it with pilgrims in this new holy land is my joy and honor. In the Old Testament, pilgrims were commanded to "go up to the Lord"—my prayer and hope is that through the Blessed Mother's apparitions, all mankind, without exception, will accept the call to "go up to the Lord" for everlasting life!

Father Slavko

8

Father Slavko

She is with us!

[In July of 1987, the author had come with her family to Medjugorje, not knowing what to expect. A letter of introduction to Fr. Tomislav Pervan, pastor of St. James, prompted Fr. Slavko Barbaric to invite her to conduct an interview. Fortunately her husband had brought a video-camera, and this interview was the result. Her experience as a lawyer had prepared her to pursue a logical line of questioning; beyond that, there was no formal preparation. Other invitations from the Visionaries soon followed, and this project was born.]

Slavko Barbaric, O.F.M., is the Visionaries' Spiritual Director, and the author of *Pray with the Heart*. English not then being one of the many languages in which he was conversant, Fr. Philip acted as interpreter.

* * *

Are the apocalyptic events a part of the Blessed Mother's message at Medjugorje?

First of all, we do not speak about the apocalyptic events in connection with Medjugorje. It is really not of primary orientation. Medjugorje has become a place of hope. The Blessed Mother says: *"I come to lead you to peace and to bring you peace."* She invites us always to fast and pray, in order to receive and achieve this very peace. Peace doesn't just mean to remove the threat of war. It does mean that it could ward off war. But peace has another dimension: it is a real state of the soul and of the heart. This state of soul helps us to love people and to really help them.

The Blessed Mother also says: *"Pray so that you can love and therefore overcome tiredness and every other type of obstacle."* The tiredness—especially the ethical, moral fatigue and the lack of endeavor—we can overcome. In a sense, every conflict, every divorce, every war is a manifestation of this fatigue. The Blessed Mother is inviting us to remedy this spiritual fatigue. Many people have understood that and have responded.

We are really walking on a new path of peace and reconciliation. This is the real content and meaning of Medjugorje.

Regarding the question of an apocalyptic dimension, certainly, we understand the possibility for catastrophe to occur. But the Blessed Mother did not come primarily to speak about catastrophes; she came to show us the way to peace. Those who see Medjugorje primarily from an apocalyptic point of view have not really grasped where she is trying to lead us.

Recalling the apparition of Fatima, there the Blessed Mother warned that there would be global war, if man did not turn back to God. World War II did occur, as she had warned. You mention a spiritual fatigue—if man does not turn back to God, will there be dire consequences?

The Blessed Mother has told the Visionaries that she would confide in them ten secrets. There are both nice and difficult things. The primary importance is the road towards peace, and this is the primary message for us. It should give us the energy and impulse to go forward. If we follow these paths, then whatever the consequences, we have the ability to avoid—

To avoid what? To possibly avert catastrophe?

Yes, to avert.

Is the Blessed Mother's path of peace, penance, fasting, conversion, prayer, and reconciliation our way to avert these catastrophes?

I'm sure of that. It depends on us. Catastrophes don't just happen from Heaven. Catastrophes are our own creation, our own preparation. The Blessed Mother is telling us to stop preparing catastrophes.

In other words, catastrophes come out of man's heart?

Catastrophes come from an unconverted heart. The biggest catastrophe is a lack of love. Once love and forgiveness are no longer available to man, anything becomes possible. For that reason our primary responsibility must be to love, forgive, and pray, and go forward. Once people start stressing the catastrophe, they harden into focusing on the catastrophe itself, rather than on the positive product of peace. The whole world could be at peace externally, but if you have a so-called "enemy," then in a sense you are at war with that person. So in that respect, we each have a part to play in what happens in the world. The Blessed Mother has said: *"I want you to love with peace and joy, and without you, nothing can happen in this world. I can't do it without you.*" So that means first peace for us from the Lord, and then peace for others.

What about drugs and alcohol?

This is an important question, and it, too, involves peace. From experience, we can say this: whoever gets involved with drugs and alcohol isn't really seeking that as a primary goal. This person is really looking for peace and a solution to a problem. These people are seduced by false paths for peace, because someone has told them that this is how you can find peace.

Also, people believe that war is the path to peace. That's another big lie; it is destruction in the mind. So, for those in trouble with drugs: pray and hope. And let us not make judgments about their situation; such judgments cause arguments. Drugs are a way of substituting for that which someone hasn't given them. When we haven't been able to succeed with someone, God is able to make a beginning. This is hope. There isn't just this world's view; there is another view. And if we don't see a solution to all the problems in this world, we know there will be a future world of solutions.

Are these solutions beyond the human mind to contemplate?

Yes.

We have heard that the Visionaries have seen Heaven, Hell, and Purgatory—would you comment?

I think they were permitted to see Purgatory so that they could witness to us. They didn't see detail; they don't really know what Purgatory is. They have described traditional views of Hell, like flaming fire;

Purgatory, like some kind of darkness, devoid of light; Heaven like a great community of love. So they are naive witnesses—"we know it exists, we saw it."

Mirjana, the oldest of the Visionaries, and Marija stated that Hell is a place a person chooses to go, that God doesn't put anyone in Hell. A person chooses Hell by rejecting God— is that true?

Yes. We already know that from our theology. God created us for Himself, and demonstrated this by sending His Son. But He created us free, and in this mysterious manner of exercising freedom, man is able to choose away from God, to reject God.

Does the Blessed Mother ever mention problems in the United States?

The Blessed Mother in her general messages has never spoken specifically about any country's problems. What she has said is valid for everyone in all countries in the world. I want to emphasize: the way of peace is possible for everybody, anywhere, because God's word is never spoken in vain. If the Blessed Mother, in Our Lord's name, invites us to peace, this presupposes it is possible for whoever hears it. And therefore, the same conversion is possible— for the old, the young, the middle-aged.

The problem of abortion is world-wide—has she spoken about that?

The Blessed Mother has spoken as the Queen of Peace. She could also have spoken as the Mother of Life, because wherever there is peace must also be life. And wherever there is true life, peace follows. War is always the destruction of life, and wherever you destroy life, there is war. So peace would solve the problem of abortion in an indirect way. We accept our life from God, and when we begin to live it with

Him, we get peace, harmony. In that way we begin to respect life in others. We can talk all we want about abortion, but if we don't begin loving life, particularly our own life in God, we will always be ready to destroy life.

Consider this: the Queen of Peace is also the Queen of Life. In this is resolved the problem of peace and abortion, for abortion is war. Every year, fifty to sixty million lives are destroyed. That is all-out war!

Continue with the thought: the Blessed Mother is the Queen of Peace. She wants to train us for life. Therefore, if we live life in union with God, we obviously live the source of life which is matrimony. And life is the very foundation of matrimony. Every divorce is a sign that we really do not accept life. Just like every abortion. If we truly convert and turn towards life in God, then after that, the other things are resolved. Many families have been reconciled among themselves after they visit Medjugorje.

What do the Visionaries call the Blessed Mother?

Someone once asked Vicka which name she preferred for the Blessed Mother—friend, sister or mother. "All three," she said, "but if I had to choose one, I would choose mother." Why? "Because when you see her, you have the impression she wants to embrace everyone in the world. Also, she wants to save everyone." For this, she is the prototype for mother. The Blessed Mother is an example to mothers and to all women. In that sense, from the viewpoint of the mother, you can explain war. Every conflict, every aggression, ultimately flows from the conflict of not being loved. The situation in the world today signifies a lack of mothering love.

When mothers love in the family, they are laying

the foundation for peace, because they are removing this lack of love. The Blessed Mother opens this way, which is possible to walk in, and in this we need a very profound conversion. When we think of abortion, we think of the hand of a mother involved: instead of loving the life within her, she makes war upon it. Even if all leaders of all countries are at peace, that mother is making war. If we let go of that and begin to love, then we begin to walk the Blessed Mother's way.

It has been said that Satan has been given the 20th Century to wage war of sorts against Christ's Church, and we have heard that the Blessed Mother said one of the ways we would see the devil's influence is through the high divorce rate—is it possible that he could be the cause?

When it gets to a question of a century belonging to Satan, we do not speak about it in that way. Satan from the very beginning has been the enemy of man. He is one who lies and one who kills. In every century, man has had the ability to either cooperate with him or resist him. The same is true today. Whenever we choose to cooperate with him, he has power. If we don't, then even in our century he does not have this power.

Does our secular culture increase his capacity to lie and deceive?

Well, who is the one who creates the culture? It's us. We do it. High technology, bombs, culture—I would repeat that if we return to the source of life, which is our life with God, then we can resolve many problems. This is in the message of the Blessed Mother, when she says that if we love one another, then we can resolve many problems. With love, we can solve even situations which seem impossible.

What about where one member of a family has received the messages and converted but others are resistant or openly hostile?

I know of families that pray the rosary together every day. That is a simple argument, that it is possible to pray the rosary. If the mother and father begin to pray themselves after many years, and the children have not prayed, I'm sure that even if they started too late, with prayer and patience, even that can be resolved. This should be a matter of comfort for parents and even priests, for priests, too, have the situation that in their own family there are not prayers. In the end, God will not demand of you why others do not pray. So we must do what we can: pray and hope that others will follow. God is patient and gives us time. Remember that, for if we become impatient with anybody, we will not succeed.

Can you give us an example?

Yes. Jelena, a young girl who has inner-locutions, has experienced the voice of the Blessed Mother, of Our Lord Jesus, and even of Satan. I asked her, "How do you know which is speaking?" She said, "Very easy: when the Blessed Mother speaks, there is an ease about it, no time pressure. You're free, literally. When Satan starts to speak, I immediately become nervous, feel pressure and urgency and feel that there is no time."

Drawing from her experience: if our love becomes strong, then we, with our own prayers, can support those who do not pray. We must not judge them or anybody else. We are not here to judge or condemn. Jesus said that judgment is for the Father. You love, and you just be a light in the world. In no message has the Blessed Mother ever said, "Go and judge the world." Just bring light and love and faith and joy.

What if you feel called to fast, and other members of your family don't?

The Lord will not ask you about the others; He just wants you to fast. Communal fasting does encourage others and makes it easier. The spirit of self-sacrifice is contagious. Often if only one family member takes the lead, the whole family will follow.

How would you describe what's happening to the Visionaries, as the Blessed Mother helps them?

The Visionaries are free. Even if they have direct teaching from Heaven, they remain free. Even in their spiritual growth. I have seen the mystery of man's freedom. This is a good thing for us. Let us start from zero: these Visionaries do have a great grace. But we have the same grace.

How so?

Because, if we respond to the messages of Medjugorje, we can grow just as the Visionaries have. I know of some young people in the parish who I think are more profound in prayer than the Visionaries. The Blessed Mother respects the rhythm of every character, every individual, and every shade of psychological development.

These Visionaries can be compared to a telephone wire: the wire stays the same. If the Visionaries do not pray, as the Blessed Mother has asked all of us to, then they remain quiet, like a wire without a message. In this I have encountered the mystery of freedom.

They also have to make their own decisions about prayer and fasting. And it is not always easy for them, either. Because they are free, I think this freedom has preserved them, in fact, from every other type of fanaticism. They are not nervous or concerned about whether people have converted or whether people are listening to the messages. They are free and just go ahead in their own rhythm and do not worry about the rest of the world. If they were not free themselves, they would not be able to contribute to us and understand our individual freedom. This is the degree of their maturity and growth. The Blessed Mother leads them. She is very patient with them. They experience this loving patience every evening. I know, therefore, they are also growing in their patience and their availability to people. But I repeat: it is not because they see the Blessed Mother, but because they have begun to do what she has asked them to do. Maybe you will understand better, if I say we are all more or less on the same level now. We all enjoy the same privilege.

Are we all to try to live the message, as these young people here are?

Yes, it is for everybody. No one should renounce or reject peace.

What about non-Catholics who do not believe in the Blessed Mother?

Believing in the Blessed Mother is not the issue; they don't have to believe in her, in order to respond. But if we will truly carry peace and love to the world, they will believe in us, as witnesses. If we begin to truly live the Blessed Mother's message, then others will accept our teacher.

Tell us a bit about prayer, Father.

The Mass is the greatest prayer. I think the power of prayer and its value does not depend on the place where you are. You can be distracted in church, and you can concentrate in your car. But obviously one prays more easily in a church. The Blessed Mother has asked us to mentally prepare for the Mass. And also to thank the Maker after Mass. Jelena said that if a person does not have time to come to church in advance, to prepare for Mass, you can start preparing in the house. As soon as you make the decision to go to Mass, ask yourself: "With Whom am I going to meet?" You are, therefore, already beginning to pray and prepare. I think you could apply the same thing after Mass. If a person is unable to remain in church, he could still leave with the wonderment of asking himself: "With Whom have I been, and what has happened to me?" This is the beginning of the continuous prayer to which the Blessed Mother invites us. She is not just asking for the movement of lips when we pray; what we call unceasing prayer does not depend on lip movement. The Blessed Mother is calling us to continuous contact with the Lord in all situations.

The Blessed Mother has encouraged us to fast on bread and water—can the spirit of mortification be substituted, or is it specifically a denial of food?

First of all, fasting has its own value—positively. Do not immediately think of mortification as denying food. Fasting is like prayer—like the two legs of a spiritual life. With fasting and prayer, we can walk on the road of holiness. All the saints, the Apostles, the Blessed Mother, have fasted and have prayed. But also, a poor person has to fast like a rich person. In fasting you begin to see more fully the things that disturb you.

You do not ask a poor man to give money to other people. But by fasting, he can become free of the aggressions which he does have. A rich person might be expected to give money to a poor man. In that sense, we can talk about renunciation for both of them. But, in spirituality, I think we are not really capable of renouncing anything. We are really only capable of choosing a better thing when we find it. If we discover love towards other people, we can without difficulty give up TV or money, because we have discovered love—a higher value. Take a dog with his favorite bone: you can not get it out of his mouth. But if you throw him a steak, he lets go of the bone immediately.

We have to discover this positive road. We are Christians—not just to fight sin, though every man must resist it. Our primary obligation, living in this world as Christians, is to demonstrate the good and flush the bad from it. When we have discovered these higher values, the battle against sin is not so difficult.

Regarding the spirit of fasting, would you elaborate on what the Blessed Mother wants?

Fasting sets us free—in our spirit and in our body. If by means of fasting, we develop a greater desire for God, then we are more free in front of material things, and there begins peace. War comes, because we are attached to some material things which we want to hold onto, or we want something that another has. By fasting, there begins to be a sort of liberation, a freeing from material desires. When you begin to live this interior freedom from exterior things, then you have no need to speak of the spirit of mortification.

It is a matter of growing spiritually. If in growing, something disturbs you, then you can put it away, leave it. For example, with the saints, it is often said they renounce their family, renounce food, live in a desert. I say no; they really do not renounce much. They follow their path towards God. It becomes a matter of course that they let go of those things— because they have a hold on them. Once you embrace God, you let go of other things, because there is no room for them anymore. So the issue is not giving up wealth or luxury: you have found something better when you have found God. God leaves no room in your life for other things.

When people are affluent, are they spiritually safe with their possessions?

Naturally, there always have been wealthy people. It is difficult for them, when they discover God. But they become less attached to what they once considered wealth. When they find God, things of the earth no longer satisfy them, and they are no longer willing to expend valuable time for mere earthly gratification.

What is the immediate goal of a prayer group?

Every prayer group has to grow in a consciousness of a pilgrimage—a walk ahead in God. For our Christian life, the criterion is not how much we pray, or how much we fast, like the Pharisees. It is peace in the heart, and love for others. This means true love for God, not just a secular humanism.

How do we grow in our prayer life?

We know we have need of purification, reconciliation, and forgiveness. And people, having discovered this life, will go to confession and pray almost as a consequence.

Regarding confession—how often should we go?

Here, the general rule is: confess every month. Again, it is not a rule, but an invitation. If we begin to live intensely with God, then as soon as we feel we have done something wrong, we go wash our hands. If we get our hands dirty, we do not have to wait a month to wash. This is a normal invitation. If a person is sick, he visits the doctor more often than if he is not sick. But healthy people also go for periodic check-ups.

How do we prepare for confession?

When we prepare for confession, do not ask what we did wrong. Ask instead: do we really love God above all in every circumstance, and love our neighbor as our self? In that regard, St. James said: "Even the just man fails seven times a day"—because we can always love more. We can love purely.

We must always grow in conversion. If we are satisfied with some *Our Fathers* and a once-a-year confession, if we act like the man who said of taxes, "The less you pay, the better you live," then we have lost the dynamic of faith, of God above all and neighbor as self.

How do we live the messages at home?

In humility. You may invite others to join you, but not in the sense of "What a prize we have got! Now come and join us!" Rather, be a light to others by your own conversion, and gently invite those around you to come and join you on the walk, the search for God, as pilgrims.

Is it true the Blessed Mother has asked us to pray three hours a day?

The Blessed Mother has asked for prayer twenty-four hours a day. Prayer without ceasing—the Biblical prescription— means to be living in a state of prayer. Jesus has called us to no less. But in her school of prayer, the Blessed Mother started very gently with us. If you were to go to someone's house and say, we must pray three hours a day, it would be a terrible mistake. Do like the Blessed Mother and start with seven *Our Fathers, Hail Mary's* and *Glory Be's*. No one can say that's too much.

If you continue, you will start finding time for the rosary, the Bible, the Mass. Remember: only after three years and three months of apparitions, did she ask for the complete fifteen decades. Only after five years and nine months, did she ask Marija's prayer group to pray before the Blessed Sacrament three hours per day. But don't be afraid to start with the seven Our Fathers. Start small, but persevere—and grow.

What is the procedure for the messages?

We used to have messages for all once a week on Thursdays. Now, the messages for the world are only on the 25th of the month. These have been immediately publicized. I would emphasize that the Blessed Mother herself gives the message. She does not give a message each day; she comes to pray with the children. There are no daily publicity releases for what occurs between them. The profound message is: she is with us! The fact that the apparitions occur before the evening Mass is itself a message, a preparation.

What is the primary focus of these apparitions at Medjugorje?

This: Jesus gave the Blessed Virgin Mary to us, through John at the foot of the Cross. And He gave us to her. She has always said yes to Him—even under the Cross, where she became our mother. And now, in this critical time, God has sent her to the world. She is here with us at Medjugorje, every day. Her message—calling us to faith, peace, prayer, penance, reconciliation, fasting and conversion—is meant to bring all her children in the world back to her Son Jesus.

Notes

1
Mirjana

[1] *The Apparitions of Our Lady at Medjugorje,* Svetozar Kraljavik, O.F.M., Franciscan Herald Press, 1984, pp. 125-26.

[2] "Hail Holy Queen, Mother of Mercy, our life, our sweetness and our hope. To thee do we cry, poor banished children of Eve. To thee do we send up our sighs, mourning and weeping in this valley of tears. Turn, then, most gracious advocate, thine eyes of mercy toward us. And after this, our exile, show unto us the Blessed Fruit of thy womb, Jesus. O clement, O loving, O sweet Virgin Mary! Pray for us, O Holy Mother of God, that we may be made worthy of the promises of Christ."

3
Vicka

[1] "Jesus said: I am the Way; I am Truth and Life. No one can come to the Father except through me." (John 14:6, NJB)

[2] "Now a great sign appeared in heaven: a woman, robed with the sun, standing on the moon, and on her head a crown of twelve stars." (Revelation 12:1)

[3] "So do not be afraid of them. Everything now covered up will be uncovered, and everything now hidden will be made clear." (Matthew 10:26)

[4] "But it is as scripture says: What no eye has seen and no ear has heard, what the mind of man cannot visualize; all that God has prepared for those who love him." (I Cor. 2:9)

[5]"Jesus replied: Anyone who loves me will keep my word, and my Father will love him, and we shall come to him and make a home in him." (John 14:23)

[6]To keep our heart pure means to keep it for God alone— keep Him first, keep Him as our goal, our source, our life, our ultimate love.

[7]A clean heart is a heart that is detached from all that is not God. A clean heart sees all things through God and with God and in God. "Blessed are the pure in heart: they shall see God." (Matthew 5:8)

6
Marija

[1]"In love there is no room for fear, but perfect love drives out fear, because fear implies punishment and no one who is afraid has come to perfection in love." (I John 4:18)

[2]"We have recognized for ourselves, and put our faith in, the love God has for us. God is love, and whoever remains in love remains in God." (I John 4:16)

7
Father Philip

[1]I Kings 18.

[2]Mal. 4:5.

[3]Matt. 17: 11-13.

[4]John 3:16.

[5]Gal. 4:4.

[6]John 12:31ff.

[7]John 19:25; Rev. 21:2ff.

[8]Rev.12:17.

Printed by Paraclete Press
Orleans, MA 02653
1-800-451-5006

This Book belongs

TO

Son Lee